SAN JUAN BAUTISTA

The Town, The Mission & The Park

by
Charles W. Clough

edited by
Bobbye Sisk Temple

Word
Dancer
Press

Sanger, California

Published by

Word Dancer Press
1831 Industrial Way, Ste. 101
Sanger, CA 93657
1-800-497-4909

Printed in the United States of America
ISBN 1-884995-07-1

Library of Congress Catalog Number: 95-61174

Second Printing June, 2004

Clough, Charles W.
    San Juan Bautista : the town, the mission & the park / by
Charles W. Clough.
    p. cm.
    Includes bibliographical references and index.
    Preassigned LCCN: 95-61174.
    ISBN: 1-884995-07-1.

1. San Juan Bautista (Calif.) -- History.   I. Title.

F868.F8C56 1995   979.4'82
                                         QBI95-20414

CONTENTS

INTRODUCTION & ACKNOWLEDGMENTS

San Juan Bautista is certainly entitled to the synonym "the City of History." That is why I undertook the task of compiling a history of the town, the mission, and the state park.

During my publishing career I published five books about families or portions of the area, but none could be termed a history such as the total San Juan Bautista deserves.

The story of the City of History embraces over two hundred years of visions and goals, successes and growth, mixed with bitter defeats and internal conflicts. The town, however, had a spirit of camaraderie to build, rebuild and go forward together.

The Indians were here first and became an important part of the mission, which was on "center stage" for forty years. As the role of the mission declined, the town began to grow. For over one hundred and fifty years the town and the mission moved forward together. The mission became a parish church, and the lay residents of the area continued a record of uninterrupted service to the parish.

The California State Park Commission in the 1920s set a goal of making California the "Grandest Playground" of the world. San Juan Bautista appealed to the commission, and a study of the town and mission ordered by the commission resulted in not one but two parks being authorized. Thus the third unit of the historic trio was established in 1935; *i.e.* the San Juan Bautista Historic Park and Fremont Peak State Park.

The trio preserves much of our heritage from the Spanish, Mexican, European, and Oriental past.

Many people and many sources were necessary in compiling this book. When information came from a primary source it has been identified. In many cases it would have been redundant to name sources of every small incident. This is true with people as it is with contemporary written sources.

Grateful acknowledgments are made for the assistance of scores of people in San Juan Bautista and Hollister.

Some were regular helpers and contributors. John Skey, who with his wife, M.L., operates the Little House shop, took charge of photographing scores and scores of pictures for the book. He also picked up material and ideas for enriching the book.

Pioneer officers of the San Juan Bautista Historical Society Richard Gularte and Georgana Gularte and several members of the society gave many hours of assistance.

The information freely supplied by Leonard Caetano was most helpful. During his forty active years in community affairs he served as mayor for sixteen years, as manager of the cement plant and as leader for many years of the fiestas, rodeos, and commemorative events.

In Hollister, Janet Brians and assistants at the Hollister Memorial Museum helped with pictures and information. The *Free Lance* newspaper and employees of the county clerk's office all helped.

The Reverend Max Santamaria and Ruth Battinich at the Old Mission Church supplied both pictures and information.

Ranger Nedra Martinez and the other rangers at the State Parks obtained a great deal of material from their Sacramento offices and made local pictures, maps, and information available.

The staffs at the San Juan Bautista City Hall as well as those of the Chamber of Commerce were most cooperative.

On my many trips to Luck Memorial Library I was warmly received by the librarians and the volunteers who staff the library. The town is very fortunate to have an organization like the Library Auxiliary, which has supported the city library for over one hundred years. I was most appreciative of the viewer, copier, and microfilm which the auxiliary and historical society jointly provided for the library when complete files of the *San Juan Mission News* became available.

The cooperation of other libraries has also been most helpful. The first contact I made for information was the California State Library in Sacramento. I was rewarded with a good general overview of available material. The Bancroft Library at the University of California, Berkeley made available the microfilm of fourteen San Juan and Hollister newspapers from 1870 and 1871.

From the library of the California State Historical Society in San Francisco I received valuable information on local Indians as well as a list of available material on the mission and town. Of special interest was the material furnished about the Malaspina Science and Art Expedition that visited Monterey County in 1791. The Indians and their homes that the artists sketched are undoubtedly the earliest likenesses ever made. Clothing was probably added at the request of the clergy. With copies and information furnished I was able to rent two of the sketches for exclusive use in this book from the Museo de America and Museo Naval in Madrid, Spain.

I was most happy when my friend Rollin Pickford offered to paint the Mission church for the cover art. He made several trips from his summer home in Santa Cruz to do his very attractive painting. Rollin is a native Fresnan but he has painted scenic areas from Hawaii to Carmel to Maine during his lifelong career.

Most of the items listed in the bibliography are available. You may also check the microfilm to see what the newspaper may have said about some events in this century which would be important to you or your family.

Most important and closer to home, I want to thank my wife, Carmen, for the many hours of travel, conversation, suggestions, ideas, translations, and loving patience during these months of research and preparation. And, a special thank you to her for many hours of typing.

As the project reaches completion, I want to acknowledge and say thank you for the contributions and help of Bobbye Sisk Temple, who edited the manuscript. Doris Hall set the type and made helpful suggestions as she has done for most of the books I have published for others in the past twenty years. And I thank my publisher, Stephen Blake Mettee of Quill Driver Books, for his patience, helpful suggestions, and a most attractive book.

Thank you all, including those helpers identified throughout the book.

Charles W. Clough
July 1995

Cover Illustrations

The front cover illustration is from a painting by Rollin Pickford. The other paintings are the work of Les Anderson who owns the Bear Flag Gallery at 207 Third Street in San Juan Bautista. We would like to thank both artists.

Photo Credits

We are indebted to the following for the photographs on the listed pages. Other photos or illustrations are acknowledged by the print or are from John Skey or the author:

San Juan Bautista Historical Society public archives:
25, 37, 38, 39, 40, 41, 42, 43, 46, 49, 50, 55, 63, 72, 76, 77, 78, 83, 84, 86, 88, 89, 91, 92, 96, 100, 101, 102, 105, 106, 108, 110, 111, 112, 113, 115.

San Juan Bautista State Historical Park:
31, 032, 35, 41, 44, 45, 51, 56, 107.

Hollister Historic Museum:
47, 79, 81.

INDIAN DAYS

hen adventuresome travelers on the El Camino Real first came to the San Juan Bautista area they found beehive-shaped houses but few Indians. The Indians would hide, preferring to be left alone to enjoy the lifestyle their ancestors had established following their arrival from the north.

The Indians who lived in this pristine valley and the nearby canyons were known as Mutsunes. There were many other Indian groups farther up the valley and known by other names. The Spanish named the Indians' living areas rancherias, a name that is still generally used.

There is no history or evidence of battles among the groups in any of the rancherias. There were codes of conduct, and if there was a serious breach, they had relatively peaceful ways of settling the differences.

THE INDIANS BEFORE

In 1967, Martin Penn, a student of California Indians, wrote a concise report on the Mutsunes' lifestyle before the arrival of white men:

Prior to the Spanish occupation of California the Mutsune Indians were in control of the San Juan Valley. One of their main village sites (rancherias) was on the eastern edge of the present city limits of San Juan Bautista. It was called 'Popelouchum.' Other rancherias were in the San Juan Canyon and in the foothills to the east and west of town.

The Mutsunes were hunters and seed-gatherers. The men fashioned spear points and arrowheads out of flint and obsidian and were accomplished in hunting and fishing. The women gathered berries and dry seeds. These were ground up in stone mortars which had been patiently hollowed out by the women.

They lived in bee-hive-shaped huts made of willow sticks and coarse grass. The women wove beautiful baskets that were water-tight. To heat water they simply filled a basket full of water and added rocks that were hot out of the fire.

The clothing of the women consisted of a brief skirt, and the men usually wore nothing at all except in winter time when they occasionally wore a cape of rabbit skins.

The Mutsunes often 'bore a grudge' against neighboring tribes such as the Ausaymas Indians of the Pacheco Pass area, but were not considered an aggressive war-like people. The last full-blooded Mutsune Indian died in January of 1930. She is buried in the Indian Cemetery beside the Old Mission Church."

INDIAN RANCHERIAS/TRIBES

The Indians of the San Benito area lived in relatively small units. Father Zephyrin Engelhardt, who, in the 1920s, authored several histories of California missions, had many volumes to draw from while compiling his history of Mission San Juan Bautista. After completing the book he added the following list of twenty-eight rancherias "mentioned in the books" he had used. They were listed in Appendix D.

Ausaime (Absayme?)
Calendarruc
Chausila
Copha-Copcha
Cuccuun-Cucunu
Cutocho
Eyulahuas
Gauchir Sierra
Guachir (Huachir) Playa
Hualquemne

Courtesy Archivo del Museo de America, Madrid, Spain
Photo Joaquin Otero

INDIANS BEFORE THE MISSION

These are rare wash drawings of 1791 made by artists on a Spanish expedition to California. They are undoubtedly two of the very earliest drawings of Monterey County Indians.

The picture above includes the unusual beehive-shaped huts made of willow branches and coarse grass by the Mutsune Indians living in the San Juan Mission area. The Indians in the coastal area were of the same stock and similar living habits.

The artists obviously exercised artistic license regarding the abundance of clothes. The two in the background of the lower picture are most correctly dressed—very little. The woman in the foreground appears to be wearing clothes for the four seasons at one time.

Alejandro Malaspina headed an around-the-world scientific expedition which was sent out by the Spanish Crown and visited the Pacific Coast in 1791. It was composed of scientists and artists, some of whom created these drawings. These two were part of fifty shown as an exhibit of the Art of the Malaspina Expedition by the California Historical Society in July 1960.

Courtesy Museo Naval, Madrid Spain

Huiñirren
Motsun-Mutsun
Nepthrinthre (th as in think)
Notoslitho
Nututhro
Oyima
Orestaco
Pagsin
Papeloutchom
Quithrathre
Silelamne
Sutusuunthre
Tamanos
Teilamne
Thrayapthre
Tulareña
Unijaima
Uthrocus

There are omissions as evidenced by a list in the program for the 1897 centennial observance of the founding of the mission. It has only eight of the above tribes plus nine more. Those formulating the list may have been assisted by Indians still alive in 1897.

The nine additional tribes, as they called them, were reported by the editor of the program:

"From the census lists I copy the names of some of the tribes of Indians, as follows: Cynlahaus, Chausita, Genche, Paucho, Cothsemejait, Achilia, Paicines, Tructa."

One friar at the mission, Father Arroyo de la Cuesta, was a recognized linguistic scholar, and by 1815 he was able to give his sermons in seven San Juan Indian dialects. He also wrote an overview of the Mutsune language which the Smithsonian Institution used as a basis for a more complete version to be kept in its archives.

THE GAMES INDIANS PLAYED

Indians are too often portrayed as warlike or as listless and slothful, but the fact is they, both men and women, were given to competitive games, many of which required speed and agility.

The 1902-03 Report of the Bureau of American Ethnology was devoted to games of the American Indians and published by the Smithsonian In-

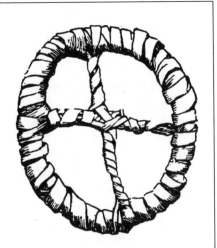

An Indian game ring three to four and a half inches in diameter, used in the game called Takersia. In some areas it was also used in competitive bow and arrow games.

A hand game called Calapooya by Wintun Indians in Monterey County was played with four bones, each two and a half inches in length. Two tied in the middle with cord and two plain ones were used in a guessing game for four players. This game is also described for Rumsen Indians, also identified as being in Monterey County. The Wintuns were identified as being of the Copehan stock and the Rumsens of Costanean stock by the American Museum of Natural History.

stitution in 1907. The book was based on reports from across the country and required 809 printed pages.

The Monterey/San Juan area was poorly reported, but we find three games detailed, all by foreign travelers. They are classified as stick games; a hand game; and a hoop and pole game. There were probably more, including almost certainly a dice game which was especially popular with the women in other nearby areas.

Stick Games

Reported by Otto Kotzebae in *A Voyage of Discovery* (1815-18), Vol. 1, p. 281, London, 1821.

This being a holiday, the Indians did no work, but divided into groups, amused themselves with various pastimes, one of which requires particular dexterity. Two contestants sit on the ground opposite each other, holding in their hands a number of thin sticks which are thrown up at the same time with great rapidity. They immediately guess whether the number is odd or even. At the side of each of the players a person sits, who scores the gains and losses. They always play for something and yet possess nothing but their clothing, which they are not allowed to stake. They employ much pains and skill to acquire little white shells, which serve instead of money.

Elsewhere it is reported:

"The game is played between two antagonists, at odd or even, with short sticks; an umpire keeps the account with other sticks."

Hoop and Pole Game

Reported by J. F. G. de la Perouse in *A Voyage Around the World in the Years 1785, 1787, and 1788*, Vol. 2, p. 223, London, 1798.

They have two games to which they dedicate their whole leisure. The first, to which they give the name of *takersia*, consists of throwing and rolling a small hoop of three inches in diameter in a space of ten square *toises* (a French unit of measure, about two yards), cleared of grass and surrounded with *fascines* (sticks). Each of the two players holds a stick the size of a common cane, and five feet long; they endeavor to pass this stick into the hoop whilst it is in motion; if they succeed in this they gain two points; and if the hoop, when it stops, simply rests upon their stick, they gain one by it; the game is three points. This game is a violent exercise because the hoop or stick is always in action.

Hand Game

The other game, named *toussi*, is more easy; they play it with four, two on each side; each in his turn hides a piece of wood in his hands, whilst his partner makes a thousand gestures to take off the attention of the adversaries. It is curious enough to a stander-by to see them squatted down opposite to each other, keeping the most profound silence, watching the features and most minute circumstances which may assist them in discovering the hand which conceals the piece of wood; they gain or lose a point according to their guessing right or wrong; and those who gain it have a right to hide in their turn; the game is five points, and the common stake is beads, and among the independent Indians the favors of their women.

Indian children liked guessing games.

One game they often enjoyed was played by using two small rocks. One rock was smooth; the other had a picture cut on it. The player closed his two fists over the two rocks. He then put his hands behind him and changed the rocks. After this he held out both hands and another guessed which hand held the rock with the picture on it. If the guess was right, the guesser took the stones in his hands. The game continued for a long time.

The boys enjoyed playing a ball game called *teekle*. The ball was made of deerskin stuffed with deer hair. It was really two balls in one, joined together in the middle. The boys divided into two teams. Each player had a stick about five feet long which he used to bat the ball. For goals they drew two straight lines about one hundred feet apart. A hole was dug in the middle of the ground for the ball. The two leaders stood by the ball and one player threw the ball into the air, and the other tried to hit it. All the boys joined in the game. The side that drove the ball over the other team's goal line won the game.

MISSION DAYS

hree periods of history are blended in modern-day San Juan Bautista.

The first is the establishment of the mission and the continued settlement of the area by the Spanish, who hoped to hold it as a new territory of the Spanish colonies. This era also included the time of rule by the Mexicans following their successful revolution. The Spanish, the padres and the Mexicans left a Hispanic legacy in the mission itself, the adobe buildings, festivals, rodeos, markets and theater.

The second period began with war, when the United States won control of California. This change caused an influx of a cosmopolitan population interested in livestock, farming and businesses to serve traders passing through San Juan, Which had become an important transportation center of California. (The town was called simply "San Juan" until 1905 when "Bautista" was added.)

The third period began in 1907 when a new spirit brought the townspeople together. The mission was repaired and the town's appearance improved. El Camino Real, still the main street of town, became the Coast Highway. Changes were made and conferences held, but it would be twenty-five years before plans matured and a California State Park was established.

Today San Juan Bautista is a community with a beautiful mission and a Hispanic legacy—a historic village with scores of well-preserved residences and businesses in a setting essentially rural.

All is complemented by two state park areas. The first is the plaza of restored buildings, with period furniture, tools, means of transportation and demonstrations of life in San Juan as it was fifty, seventy-five or a hundred years ago. The second is on Fremont Peak with facilities for picnics and camping.

It all began in 1795.

First came the Spanish padres, Franciscan Fathers under an oath of poverty and with dreams of converting and saving the immortal souls of all the hundreds of Indians in the area. The Indians would then learn the ways of the white men, the padres believed, and create pueblos just like those in Spain.

The location of the mission was determined for more prosaic reasons. Governor Diego Borica became convinced in October 1795 that it would be a great convenience to travelers if missions along El Camino Real, a public highway, were only one day's travel apart. This was not possible between Mission San Carlos (Carmel) and Mission Santa Clara, which were more than fifty miles apart.

Responding to the governor's call, a party left Monterey on November 15 to find a desirable site about midway between the two missions. The party was headed by Ensign Hermenegildo Sal and Father Antonio Dantí. They arrived at the Rio San Benito the following day and investigated the lands along the river first. They then went to the plateau west of the river, where they found a small Indian rancheria of twenty-seven cabins. The rancheria's Indian name was Papeloutchom, and it is believed to have been at the corner of Third and Mariposa streets, where the Bank of America is today. The Indians had fled, and the party saw only about six Indians at a distance.

The natural attributes of the area included plenty of timber nearby for fuel and building, tules for roofs, abundant limestone within two miles, sturdy redwoods within six miles, and adequate spring water flowing in the canyons.

The party chose a site on the bluffs overlooking the valley and the Rio San Benito. The site is believed to be exactly where the mission was later built. It was a half mile from El Camino Real, twenty-five

THE OLD
FRANCISCAN
MISSIONS
IN
CALIFORNIA.

Twenty-one missions were established in California starting with Mission San Diego, founded July 16, 1767. The twenty-first was Mission San Francisco Solano, founded July 4, 1823. Map © by Rand McNally, R.L. 95-S-220

miles from Mission San Carlos and twenty-eight miles from Mission Santa Clara.

The new mission moved closer to becoming a reality on January 12, 1796, when the Superior of Missions, Father Presidente Fermin Francisco de Lasuén, wrote to civil and church authorities for approval of this, the fifteenth mission since Father Junípero Serra had founded the first California mission in San Diego in July 1779.

Almost one hundred years earlier wealthy businessmen in Mexico had established the Pious Fund for the benefit of missions in Baja California. As the missions moved north the fund supported them eventually. (The Mexican revolution, begun in 1810, interrupted the flow of money, and litigation eventually followed which was not settled until early in the twentieth century.)

Church leaders decided in November 1796 that the new missionary outpost overlooking the Rio San Benito should be named for Saint John the Baptist, and that it should be outfitted from the Pious Fund.

It was several months before permission to build the mission came from civil authorities. The commandant of Monterey received orders to furnish a guard for the founders of Mission San Juan Bautista. The guard consisted of Corporal Ballesteros and five men. With the assistance of two workers, probably carpenters, they completed a church, missionary house, granary and guard house by June 17, 1797.

The following week Father Presidente de Lasuén came with a party for the dedication of Mission San Juan Bautista, directly from the founding ceremonies for Mission San Jose.

The dedication ceremony at San Juan, which took place on June 24, 1797 is described on the title page of the baptismal register. Following is a translation.

VIVA JESUS
First Book of Baptism of Mission San Juan Bautista, Precursor of Jesus Christ.

Founded . . . on the spot called Papeloutchom by the natives, but by our people, from the first discovery, San Benito . . .

Commenced on the very day of the Titular Patron Saint, June 24th 1797. On this day, I, the undersigned Presidente of the Missions of New California, with the assistance of the Rev. Joseph Manuel de Martiarena, and with the aid of troops destined to guard the establishment, in the presence of many pagans [Indians] from the surrounding country, who manifested much pleasure etc. I blessed water, the place and the great Cross, which we planted and venerated. I immediately intoned the Litany of All Saints, and sang High Mass during which I preached exhorting all to cooperate for such holy work. I concluded the function by solemnly singing the *Te Deum*. May all be for the greater honor and glory of God, Our Lord. Amen. Thus the place is now transformed into the Mission dedicated to the Glorious Precursor of Jesus Christ, Our Lord, Saint John the Baptist, on his very own day. Furthermore . . . I named as its first missionaries the Reverend Fathers Preachers Apostolic, Fr. Joseph de Martiarena and Fr. Pedro Adriano Martinez.

(signed) Fr. Fermín Francisco de Lasuén.

Thus, after more than a year and a half of planning, the Mission San Juan Bautista became a reality. Father Martiarena and Father Martinez had undoubtedly served in other missions in California or Mexico and knew the multiple responsibilities that faced them in addition to their ecclesiastical duties.

The friars received assistance from Mission San Carlos in the form of an experienced crew of Cumulos Indians to serve as a nucleus around which to organize and train local Indians. They, too, were entering a new world—a world that included work, any work; a world that required them to devote their time as demanded by somebody else; and a world

that offered them a new religion such as they had never known.

The workers, together with the soldiers there to protect the enterprise, were the first citizens of the town of San Juan, as it was called for many years. The mission was the dominant partner for more than thirty years.

The workers made excellent progress during the remaining months of 1797, and on December 31 the friars reported completion of an adobe chapel measuring forty-two by seventeen feet and probably covered with a tule roof; a dwelling for the missionaries, forty by twenty-five feet; a granary, seventy by nineteen feet; and a guardhouse and four houses for the mission guards or soldiers.

By the end of the second year agricultural production had increased so much that the friars built another granary, this one a hundred and forty-six by twenty-two feet, nearly twice the size of the first one. Few details about additional buildings were recorded until 1801, when the fathers were happy to report that enough tiles had been made to cover all the buildings. The missionaries' pleasure was short-lived, however, for just two years later they reported that a new granary and six houses, each twenty by fourteen feet, had been built for the soldiers, but could be roofed only with tules and straw.

The lack of tiles was a small problem when compared to the friars' accomplishments in other activities. Baptisms, the prime interest of the friars, increased from 347 in 1799 to 813 in 1801, and neophyte workers from 348 to 723. Even with totally inexperienced workers, the number of livestock increased from 1,617 to 3,285 head, and acreage planted grew from 64 to 109, resulting in increased production of grains from 676 to 3,080 bushels—a handsome growth rate for any operation in its third to fifth years.

All activities increased in subsequent years, many as much as 25 percent. Father Engelhardt, when he compiled his book in the 1920s, developed charts of each category from the best sources he could find among often conflicting records. For easy reference you will find them in appendix at the back of this book.

The major construction job, the building of the mission church began on June 13, 1806. Church dignitaries came from Monterey for the memorable event. After appropriate religious rites the cornerstone was laid and "various coins of all denomination were placed in a concavity in the first stone." The action was attested to by five of the dignitaries on a roll sealed with wax. The buildings that were completed six years later were much as they are today, nearly two hundred years later.

There being no natural rock in the area suitable for building the mission, the missionaries were obliged to make sun-dried adobe bricks, burned bricks that were baked in a subterranean kiln, and terra cotta-like roof tiles.

The adobe was made of a clay

Indians erecting Mission buildings under the guidance of the missionaries.
(From engravings by Alexander Harmer and others for Fr. Engelhardt, O.F.M.)

common to many parts of the state. It was mixed with straw and thoroughly kneaded by hand and foot. For the mission the standard adobe bricks were made thirty by sixteen by four inches and set out to dry in the sun. They were given a lime wash or stucco coating after construction was completed. The water in the canyon undoubtedly carried lime from deposits at the upper levels. The lime was responsible for bricks that have proved to be exceptionally durable.

The friars chose a site about a mile southeast of the mission for making the bricks. The clay was abundant there and a ditch brought water from San Juan Canyon. The ditch caused trouble along the Alameda in later years by frequently flooding the area. Stage companies later found the ponds convenient for washing the mud from their coaches.

The baked bricks were made of a mixture similar to adobe, but without the straw, and measured twelve by eight by two inches. They were used in arches, pillars, floors and interior areas.

The tiles were hand-molded and baked very much like the bricks. They were laid on the roof in a layer of mud about two inches thick with the tiles overlapping so an unbroken surface would face the wind and effectually shed the rain. The mud hardened and the weight of the tiles held all in place.

By the end of 1804 the friars could report that the foundations for the new church had been laid, and it would be 160 feet long and twenty-eight feet wide. They also reported that the quadrangle was nearly enclosed by a wall capped with tiles. Two years later they reported that it was completed.

In 1806 the first expedition was sent into the San Joaquin Valley to search for suitable sites for missions. A detachment of soldiers left from the San Juan Bautista mission under the command of Ensign Gabriel Moraga of the San Francisco Presidio. Father Pedro Munoz of Mission San Miguel went as chronicler. The zealous fathers were eager to win the savages for Christianity and the Spanish government was interested in spreading its presence in the area to keep it from being taken over by England, Russia or the United States.

The expedition is recorded as being the first exploration of the southern San Joaquin Valley. Moraga and his troops left the mission on September 21, 1806, and after forty-three days ended their survey 200 miles south at Mission San Fernando. Their reports were so discouraging that little more was done to find interior sites.

The records show that the missionaries feared for the safety of missions from San Miguel northward. This may be partially because of a 20 percent increase in Indian deaths in 1806. The total number of deaths amounted to 70 percent of the neophyte population, creating a shortage of laborers to maintain the mission. European diseases were the principal causes of death, but gastric problems also killed many, often from too much food, not too little.

The death rate was not destined to improve. It continued at a high rate up to 1832. Father Engelhardt's conclusion of 2,854 deaths by 1832 is supposedly based on neophytes only. This is a very high percentage if that is true, but the 2,854 falls far short of the often reported total of 4,000 to 4,500 Indians buried at the mission. There are other variances but they all add up to an unfortunate conclusion.

In the five or six years following 1806, the mission community prospered. Each of the three groups

Cemetery between the old mission church and escarpment where more than 4,000 Indians were buried.

involved—the missionaries, the soldiers and the Indians—learned their respective duties better in a pioneering effort that was new to all of them.

The missionaries were rewarded in their primary work by a regular increase in the number of baptisms to a new high in 1812 of 1,981 Indians. In the preceding six years they had baptized 11,134 Indians and sixteen whites.

The work of the religious fathers was summarized by Father Engelhardt as conducting "huge training schools which transformed indolent and ignorant savages into Christians and self-supporting members of civil society. The teachers belonged to the Franciscan Order, who, owing to their vow of poverty, could accumulate no wealth for themselves or their institute. Towards the Indian converts they stood in the capacity of fathers to their children . . .

"Through force of circumstances the missions had to be primarily agriculture, the raising of live stock, and various mechanical devices were employed on a large scale in order to produce the necessaries of life for the great patriarchal convert family."

The guards apparently were not overworked, as there are few reports of criminal activity. In 1814, an effort was made to kill missionary Father Culliboeri. The culprit was flogged, but nothing more is known about the incident.

The guards were not called upon to do any work around the mission. The houses built for them all had fenced yards, but it was critically noted that none of them ever planted gardens for extra vegetables for their families.

The neophytes, or converted *heathens*, had the most to learn and the greatest adjustments to make. Regardless of whether they were local Indians or imports from the San Joaquin Valley, they had never been obliged to work under the direction of someone else on a daily schedule.

Neophyte population averaged about 750 between 1801 and 1819, with equal division of men and women (see appendix). Housing was a continuing problem. Although small two-room houses were built for married couples, records fail to tell us just how many were needed or built.

After the mission was closed a count of 130 to 150 was used. The small huts were all adobe and the roofs, which were not maintained, quickly deteriorated.

From the beginning marriageable girls and single women were required to live in a building called the nunnery. They were free to visit their rela-

BARREL ORGAN

A barrel organ which is also known as a hand organ was given to the mission at an early date. It was made in England in 1735. The *Pacific Mutual News* of March 19, 1930 is quoted as saying it "came to San Juan the year the mission was founded." It identified the tunes on the barrels as "Go to the Devil," "Spanish Waltz," and "Lady Campbell's Hornpipe."

San Juan's famous stagecoach driver and gifted storyteller Mark Regan was more specific and told the following in an interview with historian Ralph Milliken:

"Down where the pear tree orchard used to be the Indians were camped. The men folks had just got back from the coast where they had been fishing and collecting abalones. The Indians were just eating their supper of wild herbs, onions, turnips, etc. and abalones when they looked up on the brow of the hill where the Mission now stands. They were scared at first.

"A cavalcade of strangers were up there and were unpacking their mules. It was the Mission-

The barrel organ is still at the mission but the wooden pins that produced the music are badly broken. The pipes are ornamental.

aries and their party who had come to found the Mission. They wished to secure the interest and good will of the Indians and began playing the Vals Del Diablo or Devil's Waltz on the organ.

"The Indians were delighted and came up to greet them. The Missionaries seeing them all coming towards them thought perhaps the Indians might be on the war path. So they quickly changed the tune and began playing some classical piece of perhaps Beethoven to soothe them. The Indians showed by signs that they didn't like this piece and so the missionaries started playing the Devil's Waltz again to the great delight of the Indians who came forward turning hand springs and full of glee.

"The Indians put pipes in the mouths of the visitors and showed by signs that the strangers were welcome. Among them was the chief of the Swamis Indians, the local Indians.

"These Indians stood in with the Spanish and let them have all the land on the flat. These local Indians in turn went out and brought in other Indians."

tives after their work day, but had to go to the nunnery to sleep. They were locked in by a friar, the mayordomo or a trusted neophyte.

Neophytes were free to marry following a procedure described by Father Engelhardt: "When a youth wanted a wife he would tell the missionary, who would tell him to name his intended. She would thereupon be called, and if she agreed, preparations would be made in accord with the regulations of the

church. They were given special instructions in catechism . . . Then the bans were published on three successive Sundays or holidays of obligation. On the day appointed, the couple would appear at the church, where the marriage took place before holy Mass, and during the same they received the marriage blessing and holy Communion.

"Thereupon the couple was assigned a house as their own in the village, and thereafter enjoyed the liberty and independence as full-fledged members of the Indian community. Festivities and amusements constituted a great part of the affair . . ."

He did not describe the festivities but other reports indicate that the Indians had their own dances and games, which were probably allowed at such times.

Brick by brick, tile by tile, the church was built, and in the friars' report of 1809 it was revealed that additions were being made. The church when finished would be "the widest of all mission churches in California." Father de la Cuesta wrote at year's end that "the three naves of the temple . . . were also completed this year."

"The two side naves mentioned for the first time," Father Engelhardt wrote, "must have been an afterthought; for we know that the church for which the cornerstone was blessed and laid measured but ten *varas* in width." (A *vara* is 33.07 inches, so the church was to have been twenty-seven and a half feet wide.) The new plan made the church not only the largest, but also the only mission church with two side naves.

Construction was delayed when heavy rains and an earthquake combined to cause the collapse of walls in the yard and garden.

Considering the zeal with which the friars built, the completion of the church was casually noted.

On December 31, 1812, Fathers Ullibarri and de la Cuesta informed the governor and mission President Father Estevan Tapis that the church was finished and blessed during the year. No details were given.

An entry in Book One of Baptisms, page 126, gives little more evidence that there had been any celebration befitting a task that had taken fifteen years from the day the mission was founded. The event was recorded as follows:

On the 23rd day of the month of June, in 1812, during the reign over Spain of our Monarch, Don Fernando VII (God keep him many years), and during the rule as Viceroy and Governor of Captain General Francisco Venegas, Lieutenant-Colonel Don José Joaquin de Arrillaga being Governor of this Province of Alta California, the Very Rev. Fr. Estevan Tapis being Presidente of these Missions, and the Rev. Fathers Felipe Arroyo de la Cuesta and Roman Fernandez Ullibarri being the missionaries in charge of this mission of San Juan Bautista, there was celebrated the Blessing of the new church, at which solemnity the Rev. Missionary Fathers of missions San Francisco, Santa Clara and San Jose assisted. The Patron was Don Manuel Gutierrez, citizen of the Pueblo de los Angeles of this Alta California. In witness whereof we sign. Fr. Felipe Arroyo de la Cuesta—Manuel Gutierrez.

Some have been critical of the construction time, but fifteen years was not long considering the primitive tools used, inexperienced workmen, multiple duties, sickness and earthquakes. The builders should be "commended and rewarded with our reverend appreciation of their work."

The friars may very well have been concerned by threatening clouds of discord.

Members of the Spanish Cortes (governing body) were considering secularization because progress was going more slowly than they had expected when they approved funding for the expansion into California. They had thought the savages would be quickly converted and would change their way of living so the missions would develop into pueblos or Spanish villages within ten years, but it wasn't happening. Neophyte deaths were mounting at a terrible rate per year. The revolution in Mexico presaged a variety of events, some of which would likely be welcomed by the missionaries.

The Spanish government in 1812 asked its civil and ecclesiastical units to supply answers to thirty-six questions about the Indians under their control. Communications being what they were in those days, it was 1814 before the mission fathers received and answered their inquiries. The questions were answered by Father Felipe Arroyo de la Cuesta, writing on behalf of the missionaries. The original inquiry and answers are in the archives of the Santa Barbara mission. They were translated by Father Engelhardt, who published only the answers, believing the questions were obvious.

The answers of Father de la Cuesta were naturally weighted in favor of the goals of the government and the missionaries. Many of the answers, however, give us the best contemporary descriptions of the Indians' lives in the California missions of 1814 and of their earlier way of life.

An insight into Indian health care was part of the missionary's report. He said they shared their limited supply of medicines with the neophytes. "These poor people know nothing about medicine. They, indeed, cure themselves once in a while with herbs and roots which from experience they know to be beneficial. There are many healers and sor-

Ripe olives were dumped into the mission's mill and crushed by a burro powered wheel. The resulting oil was used for cooking and lamps

cerers who win many beads [Indian money] for curing, and at other times nothing. They have the greater portion of the people deluded. They care for the Indians by singing and with gestures, and shouts making their superstitious cures. The only case in which they succeed is in bleeding with a flint, and sucking the blood.

"Likewise, in the overeating, which resulted in distress and indigestion, they apply to the patient a sort of a syringe. The most common maladies are consumption, *morbo galico* [probably syphilis], and dysentery from which many die. In a year the number of deaths exceeds that of the births."

The eating habits of the neophytes were obviously responsible for many of their health problems. In a lighter vein it was often said that "the Indians eat only one meal a day because they eat at all hours when not filled up or at work." The mission had a weekly slaughter when fifty or sixty steers were killed for the mission's total needs. At that time the Indians were allowed to eat until they could eat no more. This resulted in indigestion and probably dysentery. Unless they were very hungry, they did not like to eat the jerked beef available to them during the rest of the week.

Their daily diet included about two pounds of *atole*, a cooked cereal, for both breakfast and supper. At midday they were served a combination of wheat, beans, peas and other vegetables, either mixed or separately.

The missionaries also reported that the Indians kept a supply of acorns and wild seeds in their little cabins. "They will not let a chance pass by to catch rats, squirrels, moles, rabbits and other animals, which they were wont to eat."

Father de la Cuesta also wrote that what pleased the neophytes most were watermelons, sugar melons, pumpkins, spices and corn. He said pagans did not understand agriculture at all but even after they gained some knowledge of it they preferred what the land yields without cultivation.

"The missionaries early established a cemetery beside the mission overlooking the Camino Real and San Benito River. Several thousand neophytes were buried there with the Roman ritual." In one of their reports the missionaries gave a fairly complete description of the prior funeral practice of the Indians: "In paganism the bodies, after the spine was broken and the bodies doubled up like a ball, were interred by the relatives of the deceased in a deep hole. As soon as the pagan died, the wailing began with a most dismal chant; this was continued through two successive nights, all having their faces painted.

"The nearest relatives of the deceased would cut their hair with a sharp stone or burning stick. They

Tallow was in demand for manufacture of soap and candles and for trading. Fat from the steers was cooked over low heat in large pots like the above. As the fat melted, it was stored in large skin bags.

would deprive themselves of every ornament of the neck, ears and noses. They would also take all the wearing apparel from the dead and scatter the shreds at some distance from the rancheria. Sometimes they would invite the friends of the deceased, and regale with beads those who did the wailing, who then agreed to lament for the dead a third time."

In answer to a question about Indian character, Father de la Cuesta wrote: "The vice and pleasure most dominant in the Indians is indolence, which is

The Indians used mortars with stone pestles for grinding grains and nuts

followed by stealing, inconstancy and the remembrance of wrongs for revenge, to which they are or were extremely inclined. . . . The women are more fond of work, but they equal the men, if they do not surpass them, in the rest of the vices.

"In general, these Indians are peaceful, but they are also irascible and haughty," he continued. "The latter are those who were wont to go to war for motives and causes which are not known, but it is from immemorial." According to de la Cuesta, many had improved because of the missionaries' teachings, "notwithstanding that the weeds are not lacking in the good wheat."

In other answers Father de la Cuesta spoke of the Indians' knowledge of their origin and their belief in the hereafter. He said that they believed that their ancestors came from the north, but that their "history amounts to ridiculous fables, which are passed from generation to generation, and who relate them only for the purpose of passing time, laughing, or to entertain the boys. There was some true origin, but it became obscured in such a way that what they contain are but stories and fables.

"The whole scientific knowledge of these people consists in the better way of telling the stories or greater aptitude in hunting and fishing.

"These people had scarcely any idea of the soul, nor its immortality; nevertheless they would say that when an Indian died, his spirit would be in sacred places which sorcerers still have for the purpose of asking pardon of the devil . . . Others would say the spirits of the dead went to the west; but they could not tell what they did there. For this reason they never named the dead. Indeed, it is the greatest grief and injury even to name the dead before them; and the pagans still observe the foolish custom."

The reports gave details regarding the supervision and control of the mission. Four men served as civil officials, identified as two *alcaldes* and two *regidores*. They supervised the laborers and managed the belongings of the mission.

"These and all the neophytes in criminal matters are subject to the *commadante* of the nearest presidio; but in economical and administrative matters they are subject to the missionary fathers of the mission, who treat all as fathers treat their children, and they prepare them so that in due time they may make the said elections according to the regulations of the law."

The Indians were very fond of music and song. They learned new tunes and songs with facility, but the missionary fathers regretted that they also remembered their pagan tunes. There were many of these for various purposes. Some songs were for games, but the ones for men were different from those for women. They had songs for funerals, for periods of illness, for wartime, for the chase, for men's dances, for women's dances, for entertaining the boys (no mention of girls), for counting and for fables. Songs were sad or cheerful depending on circumstances.

THE MISSION OF MUSIC

San Juan Bautista Mission was destined to be the "mission of music" on February 13, 1815, when Fr. Estevan Tapis was assigned to the mission. He had recently retired as Padre Presidente of the California Missions and had served in California missions for twenty-five years.

He came to assist Fr. de la Cuesta, but he was about sixty years of age at the time and was not called upon to do heavy work. He was therefore able to devote much of his time to music, for which he had great talent. He also had an understanding of the Indians, whom he loved, and undoubtedly was successful with them for that reason.

To better teach the Indians' choir, he developed a different, possibly unique method of writing the music. He used large sheets for music (two by three feet) and made the notes in different shapes and in four colors: red, yellow, black and white. Four groups of Indians in the choir learned to sing their color-designated notes. Half notes were Gregorian squares, and one quarter notes were diamond shaped. The large sheets upon which the music was inscribed were of parchment made of treated sheep skin.

Fr. Tapis accomplished a great deal in his ten years from 1815 to 1825 at the mission. Fr. Engelhardt tells of how Fr. Tapis' music was used in other missions. At one mission a band was organized by the musically inclined priest. In the Santa Barbara Mission, students formed a choir to sing from the notes on pages still to be found in that mission's museum. Fr. Engelhardt also pointed out that after 1810 the missions received nothing from Spain and this added to the importance of the leadership and work of Fr. Tapis.

There is no way of evaluating the problems Fr. Tapis had in teaching the music to the totally unschooled Indians. Great patience was necessary. The Indians may have been better students than he realized. Indians had their own songs which they were delighted to sing at every opportunity, and they had different songs for each opportunity. They also may have been eager students, if the time for singing released them from arduous hours of field work.

The children were quicker to learn than the parents and often sang the choir's songs any place and any time. The older Indians were able to learn in this manner and join in the singing. It should be remembered that in 1925 there were thirteen Indian dialects spoken at the mission. Both Latin and Spanish were entirely different languages, which only a few Indians learned to any degree.

While the children learned the songs, some of the men were interested and learned to sing High Masses. It was probably men whom Fr. Tapis had taught who were involved in a story of unusual loyalty about ten years after the good father had died.

In the late 1830s some newcomers to San Juan Bautista brought whisky to sell to the Indians, which had previously not been permitted. As in many places, the Indians in the San Juan area fell victim to uncontrolled alcoholism as quickly as their parents had fallen victims to the European diseases. The Indians found it especially difficult on Saturday to abstain from drinking so much that they were not able to sing the High Mass on Sunday.

One Saturday a group of the Indian men came to Fr. Francisco and said, "Padre, we want to sing in the choir tomorrow." The priest expressed his pleasure and welcomed them to be in the choir the next day. The Indians replied, "But Father, we cannot unless you lock us up so we can't get any liquor." Fr. Francisco was pleased that the men were so eager to sing, and he agreed and locked the men in one of the church rooms and fed them. The next day they sang, and both the men and the pastor were happy, so happy in fact that they did this many times in the future so that the men would be able to sing on Sunday.

Fr. Tapis' death was mourned by many when he died on November 3, 1825. The burial register had much to say of his successful work in the other missions as well as at San Juan, and part of it said, "When he could, he would teach the boys the rudiments of ordinary school life; he would write the music for the singers in the church, by which means he endeavored to elevate the festivities and solemnness so as to attract devotion, worship and veneration in the solemnity not only among the Indians, but also among all others."

Fr. Tapis remains were buried beneath the floor of the chancel. The exact spot was unknown for fifty years. In 1875 Fr. Closa discovered the remains when repairing the floor. He had the place marked by a marble slab with appropriate inscriptions. It is within the chancel on the lefthand side.

Their instruments for the dances were described as "little sticks at the top end of which there is a sort of hollow ball containing tiny stones or gravel, the shaking of which produces noise. These rattles they shake in dancing around in a circle and at the same time they shout and yell in accord with the rattle. Sometimes they use the bones of a goose or deer with which they produce a shrill whistle.

"All or most of the dancers paint themselves in the most grotesque manner, fasten rare plumage in their hair or neck and shoulders in imitation of the most horrible figures of bears, coyotes, etc."

The last question dealt with the dress of the neophytes. "It consists of a blanket, a breechcloth, which serves the men to cover themselves decently instead of trousers, and the overall or coton. All this is manufactured at the mission. The vaqueros and the principal men wear trousers, stockings, shoes and hats. The pagans do not understand the use of dress; the most they have is a cape of rabbit or seal skins. Their women for the sake of inborn decency wear a handful of fibres of rushes or tules or a piece of deerskin. In cold weather they will cover themselves with the hide of deer. Commonly, however, the men go about entirely naked."

The answers were signed: Mission San Juan Bautista, May 1st, 1814. Fr. Felipe Arroyo de la Cuesta.

Apparently no question was asked about how Indians in the San Joaquin Valley were recruited or runaways returned to the mission. This was for the most part left up to the soldiers, guardians of the mission.

The original colored sheet music used by Fr. Tapis to teach the mission Indians to sing is on display in the mission museum.

Most reports tell us that by twentieth-century standards the soldiers treated the Indians very harshly or cruelly. If the mission fathers learned of mistreatment there was probably little they could do about it, especially after 1811. The troops were under military, not ecclesiastical, control.

California and its missions were well removed from the political turmoil and military action in Mexico's rebellion against Spanish rule. Although the revolt began September 16, 1810, there were destined to be twelve long years of fighting and negotiations before Mexico won its freedom.

The revolution resulted in the need for financial support for the missions, which were cut off from both the Spanish and Mexican governments, for items that could not be produced at the missions. From the earnings of the Pious Fund, each missionary received four hundred dollars annually for his special projects or the needs of the church. The missionaries ordered what they wanted from the College Procurator in Mexico. The articles ranged from replacement garments to trinkets for the children. These added a welcome variety to mission routine and were known as *memoria*.

Much of what the military and civil employees received came in the form of food, clothes, tools and other personal items from Mexico in lieu of cash. This placed a double burden on the missions. Most of the missions, especially San Juan, were able to grow grains, vegetables and livestock, and the demand was great. They soon learned that the drafts from the governor traded for produce "proved to be so many scraps of worthless paper from which nothing could be realized."

To get necessary tools and equipment, the missions soon resorted to barter with ships coming to Monterey. They were permitted to do this only with Spanish ships. While hides and tallow were usually the basis for barter by the missions, one exchange in 1815, approved by the governor, included flour and wool. It was reported by the friars in their year-end report: "With the product of one hundred and fifty *arrobas* [twenty-five pounds] of flour which was delivered by order of the governor of this province, and with the tallow and some wool sold to the supercargo of a Spanish corvette, this mission obtained some ploughshares, pickaxes, crowbars, iron, five small kettles and one large kettle and other necessary articles."

A piece of timber with an iron point constituted the plough of mission days.

Barter was also used on the local level. When the main altar of the mission needed to be painted, a local painter named Chaves wanted six *reales* (about seventy-five cents) a day to paint it, but the friars didn't feel they could afford that much. When Thomas A. Doak of Boston (later baptized as Felipe Santiago) arrived in San Juan, he agreed to do the job in exchange for his meals. Doak arrived in Monterey as a member of the crew of the ship *Albatross*. He deserted the ship and became the first American settler in California.

The missionaries were often able to make cash sales to vessels in addition to bartering. In the 1820s they were slaughtering cattle for mission consumption at the rate of about 2,700 per year. They were able to sell the hides for about one dollar each, but there was less demand for the tallow, and the price fluctuated. Tallow was also in demand locally for making soap. In fact, the first commercial venture in the area was an independent soap-making factory.

Through the years adobe homes with tile roofs were built for the neophytes at the rate of nineteen or twenty annually. The friars also received necessary equipment for the church from time to time, but they did not identify them as gifts or purchases, and their source is unclear.

Despite desertions and a high death rate in the 1820s, the mission was able to maintain a stable population of Indian workers. After Mexico took over the government in 1822, the missions were still required to supply the needs of the soldiers, civil employees and even some landowners.

In 1822 Father de la Cuesta wrote an informal note that has supplied information on the management of the mission which was never included in annual reports. The mission, like other ranch operations, had a mayordomo or overseer in charge of the workers. The note said that since November 1817, Joaquin Soto had held the position at San Juan. The first year he received eight *pesos* (one dollar) a month plus food. His wages were raised the next year to nine pesos plus a young bull, seven *fanegas* (about 1.6 bushels) of corn, four pesos worth of beans, eighteen tallow candles and four pesos worth of soap from the mission's own soap factory. He also was assigned an Indian assistant. He continued in the position until 1825.

Life at Mission San Juan Bautista was changed very little in 1822 when Spanish rule ended and Mexico, as victor in its revolution, took over. In fact, for a year the Spanish governor continued in office.

It was not until October 1825 that a native-born Mexican was named governor. He was Jose M.

Echeandia, who, according to Father Engelhardt, "endeavored to make the hard life of the missionaries unbearable." He was credited with "being of the Liberal School of Thought, which was infected with Voltarianism."

On January 1, 1826, Governor Echeandia issued a proclamation that was both good and bad news for the missions. He announced that everyone had to pay 10 percent of their income to support the military, a burden that until then had fallen largely on the missions. The bad news was that the missions also would have to pay the 10 percent.

Father Arroyo de la Cuesta was senior missionary at that time as Father Estevan Tapis had died on November 3, 1825. A replacement was named but sometime during the year he was transferred.

These were indeed trying times as revealed in an anguished letter written by Father de la Cuesta on August 10, 1826. The letter was to the collector of revenues at Monterey and read:

I see your application for supplies of all kinds in behalf of the troops. Some of the articles are not on hand. There are difficulties all around and I am overburdened with cares which render life wearisome. There is hardly anything of the Religious in me, and I scarcely know what to do in these troubled times. I made the vows of a Friar Minor; instead, I must manage temporalities, sow grain, raise sheep, horses and cows. I must preach, baptize, bury the dead, visit the sick, direct the carts, haul stones, lime, etc. These are things incompatible, thorny, bitter, hard, unbearable. They rob me of time, tranquility, and health of both the body and soul. I desire with lively anxiety to devote myself to my sacred ministry and to serve the Lord.

The padres did have problems. On the one hand was the changing government that looked to the missions to produce enough so Alta California could be self-sufficient.

On the other hand the missions needed workers and the principal source of labor was the Indians, not an unlimited source. For most of the 1820s San Juan mission reported nearly a 10 percent annual death rate. This was only among the neophytes; the rate among the pagans was probably as high or higher.

By 1820 the local Indians, who had been very susceptible to European diseases, were a small but loyal force. Indians then had to be brought from ever more distant places in the Tulares or farther north in the San Joaquin Valley.

The valley Indians were called Tulares. Their lives were more disrupted than the lives of the local Indians had been. They not only had to adjust to a new lifestyle, but also to a big change in climate, food and family.

This all contributed to a spirit of rebellion which was usually expressed by their running away, stealing horses (a favorite food for them) and other things of value. (Indians had mostly traded freely with each other, not understanding the idea of private property and therefore not knowing the idea of stealing.) The military guard would pursue them and

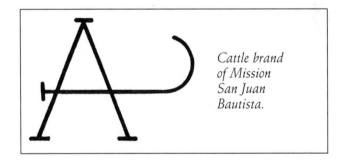

Cattle brand of Mission San Juan Bautista.

bring back both men and animals from a hundred miles or more away. The soldiers were often assisted in these hunts by loyal neophytes.

A Monterey woman whose father had been brought from Los Banos to the mission told historian Ralph Milliken in 1929 that "those in charge would send native soldiers over to catch the wild Indians." She said they used native soldiers because they knew better than the Mexican soldiers how to catch the Indians. They would catch a lot of Indians and "tie their thumbs together with strips of rawhide thongs ... in a long line tied to a man on horseback who sometimes rode at a gallop."

Another story of the Tulares is of a lighter nature. One day a large group of Tulares became aroused and came toward the mission yelling and waving their arms in a threatening way. Knowing their love of music, someone brought out the old hand organ and started turning out tunes. The Indians soon responded to the music and an amicable conclusion was arrived at.

The burden of greater production fell heavily on the field workers as well as on Father de la Cuesta, who signed the 1826 year-end report alone. He had no assistant yet.

Activities slowed although reports indicate little drop in the number of neophytes and an increase in the number of Indian marriages and baptisms. There was no report made in December 1827, or it has been lost. On January 8, 1828, however, a special report was filed and Father Felipe Moreno signed it along with Father de la Cuesta. The report supplied details of mission lands, livestock, resources, Indians and neighbors. Little activity was reported in 1829 when Father de la Cuesta was again alone.

On February 9, 1830, Father Commisary Prefect Sarria wrote to Governor Echeandia: "At Mission San Juan Bautista the missionary Father is so incapacitated that, when there is necessity of hearing a confession or administering Extreme Unction in the Indian village, he has to be bourne to the place on a stretcher. Even so he cannot visit the outside ranchos, so that I myself at times attend the sick." This caused the governor to send help, and Father Moreno returned as an assistant.

On March 20, 1829, the Mexican Congress decreed that all Spaniards in California must leave the country within three months. There was considerable opposition to the law, and the governor felt it would be unwise to exile all the Franciscan missionaries, most of whom were aged. The law was amended to exclude all Spaniards over sixty years of age—most of the Franciscans were in that age range.

The law had an adverse effect in another way. Spaniards of any age could not hold public or military office, and many, deprived of a livelihood, were forced to leave.

The civil and military offices were then filled with untrained young people whose primary qualification was that they were born in Mexico or California. These young people had little concern for the missions or the Indians. Their primary concern was their own life, land and fortune. As in many new governments, there was a great deal of jockeying for power and benefits. Although this makes for interesting reading, its limited involvement of Mission San Juan Bautista does not justify including all the details here.

The last report of Mission San Juan Bautista was signed and filed by Father de la Cuesta and Father Felipe Moreno, December 31, 1832.

The Mexican government asked the Franciscan College of Guadalupe, Zacatecas, which was all-Mexican, to take charge of the California missions. The college declined to replace the missionaries abruptly and appointed a committee to investigate

Governor Jose Figueroa and the Zacatecan Franciscans land at Monterey, January 15, 1833. The party included Fr. Jose Antonio Anzar, who replaced Fr. Juan Moreno at the Mission May 30, 1833.

W.T. Genns Collection

the situation. Father Mariano Sosa headed the group and visited the missions. As a result of his report, the colleges of San Fernando de Mexico and Guadalupe, Zacatecas agreed to accept the responsibility for the ten missions in northern California.

Father Jose Antonio Anzar was named resident missionary at San Juan Bautista. Father de la Cuesta retired to Mission San Miguel.

The first Zacatecan Franciscans arrived at Monterey on January 15, 1833. Father Anzar arrived at San Juan soon after. Records fail to tell how the change affected the Indians, 529 males and 396 females, working at the mission at the time. There was little change in their religious life, but government regulations and new laws would significantly affect them.

A law was passed August 17, 1833, that required immediate secularization of the mission. Some changes were obtained by local officials, but the law's final result was the end of the mission system.

Franciscan missionaries endeavored to win ownership of some lands for the Indians, but they found little support among officers of the new government. The Indians were not broadly trained in either government or farming. There were records of some who took up small acreages, but it apparently was not done according to the law. When whites obtained land grants, they often let the Indians remain on the land, but before long the Indians would leave to work elsewhere or return to the life of their forefathers, as much as was possible. Most local Indians had died, so it is probable that the Indians remaining at the mission were almost all from the Tulares or the San Joaquin Valley.

Writing within fifty years of secularization, several historians detail what might be called a first-hand overview of the plight of the unfortunate Indians and shed light on the entire confused situation. The following is a sampling.

A MELANCHOLY PICTURE

From the *1882 History of San Benito County*:

This mission was secularized in 1834; its cattle slaughtered for their hides and tallow; its sheep left to wolves; its horses taken by dandies; its Indians left to hunt acorns, while the wind sighs over the grave of its last padre.

This melancholy picture is not too highly colored. Doubtless the secularization laws were not intended to benefit the Indians of the missions, nor does it seem that they were conceived in a spirit of unfriendliness to the padres. But it cannot be denied that their execution resulted most disastrously to the objects of the government's solicitude. This did not result from the spirit, or imperfections of the laws, but rather from the manner in which they were executed.

Those who were entrusted with, or usurped the political power in California, and who were charged with the execution of the secularization laws, were neither wise nor overhonest. Had they reflected a moment, they could not have failed to perceive that the bond that tied the Indian to the padres was of a character that could not be severed at a moment's notice. The Indians bore unbounded affection and devotion to the friars. Simple, and of little mind as they were, they had always learned to place the same degree of confidence in the priests that a child reposes in its parents; and when the hour of separation came, their grief was unbounded and sincere. Never was the comparison of the priest and his disciples to the shepherd and his flock

This woman's name is lost to time but she has long been known as the last Mutsun woman at the mission.

more apt than in the case of the friars and the Indians.

From Thodore Hittell's *History of California, Vol. II*, P. 189:

Such were the principles and the method adopted for secularization. . . . Though it required some years to finish the ruin of the missionary establishments, this was the commencement of it. As for the Indian pueblos (the Indian villages after the confiscation were so called) which were to take their place, there was no success in any of them. Nor was any to be expected. In other cases it has required hundreds of years to educate savages up to the point of making citizens, and many hundreds to make good citizens. The idea of at once transforming the idle, improvident and brutish natives of California into industrious, law-abiding and self-governing town people was preposterous.

CONCERNED ADMINISTRATOR

A letter addressed to Governor Figueroa on December 19, 1834, by Antonio Buelna, one of the seven legislators included:

> Having executed the order of Your Honor communicated to me under date of October of the present year, when I proceeded to secularize Mission San Juan Bautista, converted it into a free pueblo, and notified all the inhabitants thereof. I also herewith bring it to the knowledge of Your Honor that, however agreeable to the Indians of the Tulares, it is impossible for me to give them complete liberty because of the indolence and incapacity which I encounter in them to be maintained by themselves along, excepting some who can be free, leaving the rest in the way and subjection in which they were before. All of which etc. . . .

CONCERNED PADRE

A month later Father Anzar wrote the governor with a long list of complaints and needs for the mission and himself. About the Indians he wrote:

> Let us consider another matter. I hold that the question of conversion of the pagans continues alive. Although they may secularize the missions, yet that does not end the matter. In the regulations I have not seen anything to the contrary. Rather, I understood that if any pagans should come, all the missionary would have to do, in order to be able to teach and catechize them, would be to ask the mayordomo to provide them each with a blanket or shirt, and the breechcloth, so that they might appear all clothed, and after baptism turn them over to the person named by the government. However, this has not been observed.
>
> About fifteen days ago as many as ten pagans, old and young together, reached here. I myself put them in charge of some other pagans who had been here, telling them that they should bring to me the two orphan girls and boys, whom they told me some had with them. They brought them; but scarcely did the mayordomo learn this, who had just arrived at the mission village, when he himself in person went and brought the two orphan girls and two orphan boys to his own house. I do not know whether he has reported this, nor had he the courtesy and good manners to tell me anything about the matter.
>
> Signed: Fr. José Antonio Anzar.

The mission era had ended. The church continued to serve its people. The records indicate some Indians remained in the area and in the church. During the next twenty-one years nearly six hundred Indians were baptized and nine hundred died.

From *Tree Years in California* by the Rev. Walter Colton, 1846:

> California, though seemingly young, is piled with the wrecks of the past, around the stately ruin [the mission] flits the shade of the padre; his warm welcome to streaming guests still lingers in the hall, and the loud mirth of the festive crowds still echoes in the darkened arches. But all these good, olden times are passed—their glorious realities are gone—like the sound and sun-lit splendors of the wave, dashed and broken on the remorseless rock.

THE RANCHO DAYS

fter the secularization of the Mission there followed a period of about ten or twelve years often referred to as the Rancho Days. The hundreds of acres that had been devoted to mission use became available for acquisition by Mexicans through government grants or purchase. This was a new world, and many people wanted a share in it by becoming land owners in the fertile valley and wooded hills.

But what of the Indians? The mission church could not care for them. The government had no program to help them. By this time, many of the Indians had known no other life-style than mission life. They were poorly prepared for returning to their tribal home, which might be as far away as one hundred miles to the east in the San Juan Valley.

Some found menial jobs. A few tried to work the land on their own, but they were not schooled in managing their own affairs. Some land owners allowed them to try, and some hired them to work as they had at the mission, but there was no way the Indians could return to the life they had known prior to mission days. The era of the Indian had ended. These were Rancho Days.

We have an exceptional description of life in the area in the memoirs of General W. T. Sherman, Who came to San Juan from Monterey in company with Lieutenant (later General) Edward O. C. Ord. Although the visit was at the end of the era, much of the content tells graphically of life in the Rancho Days. He wrote:

> . . . a mixed set of Americans, native Mexicans, and Indians. . . were kind and pleasant, and seemed to have nothing to do, except such as owned ranches in the country for the rearing of horses and cattle. Horses could be bought at any price from four dollars up to sixteen, but no horse was ever valued above a doubloon or Mexican ounce (sixteen dollars). Cattle cost eight dollars fifty cents for the best, and this made beef net about two cents a pound, but at that time nobody bought beef by the pound, but by the carcass.

> Game of all kinds—elk, deer, wild geese, and ducks—was abundant; but coffee, sugar, and small stores, were rare and costly.

> The people were very fond of riding, dancing, and of shows of any kind. The young fellows took great delight in showing off their horsemanship, and would dash along, picking up a half-dollar from the ground, stop their horses in full career and turn about on the space of a bullock's hide, and their skill with the lasso was certainly wonderful. At full speed they could cast their lasso about the horns of a bull, or so throw it as to catch any particular foot.

> These fellows would work all day on horseback in driving cattle or catching wild-horses for a mere nothing, but all the money offered would not have hired one of them to walk a mile. The girls were very fond of dancing, and they did dance gracefully and well. Every Sunday, regularly, we had a *baile*, or dance, and sometimes interspersed through the week.

> I . . . well recall [when] Ord and I . . . got permission and started for . . . San Juan Bautista. Mounted on horses, and with our carbines, we took the road by El Toro, . . . a prominent hill around which passes the road to the south, following the Salinas or Monterey River . . . It was quite dark when we . . . reached a small adobe house on the banks of the Salinas, where we spent the night. The house was a single room, without floor or glass; only a rude door, and window with bars. Not a particle of food but meat, yet the man and woman entertained us with the language

of lords, put themselves, their house, and everything, at our 'disposition,' and made little barefoot children dance for our entertainment. We made our supper of beef, and slept on a bullock's hide on the dirt floor. In the morning we crossed the Salinas Plain, about fifteen miles of level ground, taking a shot occasionally at wild-geese, which abounded there, and entering the well wooded valley that comes out from the foot of the Gavillano.

We had cruised about all day, and it was almost dark when we reached the house of Senor Gomez, father of those whom [we knew] at Monterey. His house was a two-story

was fat and old, was not over cordial. However, we sat down, and I was helped to a dish of rabbit, with what I thought to be an abundant sauce of tomato. Taking a good mouthful, I felt as though I had taken liquid fire; the tomato was *chile colorado*, or red pepper, of the purest kind. It nearly killed me, and I saw Gomez's eyes twinkle, for he saw that his share of supper was increased. I contented myself with bits of meat, and an abundant supply of tortillas. Ord was better case-hardened, and stood it better.

We staid at Gomez's that night, sleeping, as all did, on the ground, and the next morn-

A horse race in pastoral California. Physical labor had no charms for the Californian of the pastoral days, but he was fond of riding and performed most of his tasks while in the saddle. He was especially attached to his horse, and frequent contests grew out of the rivalry between the young bloods regarding the merits of their respective steeds.

(An anonymous painting in M. H. De Young Museum, c. 1920)

adobe, and had a fence in front. It was situated well up among the foot-hills of the Gavillano, and could not be seen until within a few yards. We hitched our horses to the fence and went in just as Gomez was about to sit down to a tempting supper of stewed hare and tortillas. We were officers and *caballeros* and could not be ignored. After turning our horses to grass, at his invitation we joined him at supper.

The allowance, though ample for one, was rather short for three, and I thought the Spanish grandiloquent politeness of Gomez, who

ing we crossed the hill by the bridle-path to the old Mission of San Juan Bautista. The Mission was in a beautiful valley, very level, and bounded on all sides by hills. The plain was covered with wild-grasses and mustard, and had abundant water. Cattle and horses were seen in all directions, and it was manifest that the priests who first occupied the country were good judges of land. It was Sunday, and all the people, about a hundred, had come to church from the country round about. Ord was somewhat of a Catholic, and entered the church with his clanking spurs

The Carrera de Gallo *(snatching the rooster). A rooster would be covered with loose earth, having only his head exposed. The rider then at full gallop would seize the fowl by the head without slowing down. It was also reported that a horseman at San Jose won a wager that he could start at full gallop with a tray of a dozen wine glasses filled to the brim and run fifty yards, stop suddenly and deliver the wine without the loss of a drop.*

(Coy's Pictorial History of California)

and kneeled down, attracting the attention of all, for he had on the uniform of an American officer. As soon as church was out, all rushed to the various sports. I saw the priest, with his gray robes tucked up, playing at billiards, others were cock-fighting, and some at horse-racing. My horse had become lame, and I resolved to buy another. As soon as it was known that I wanted a horse, several came for me, and displayed their horses by dashing past and hauling them up short. There was a fine black stallion that attracted my notice, and, after trying him myself, I concluded a purchase. I left with the seller my own lame horse, which he was to bring to me at Monterey, when I was to pay him ten dollars for the other. The Mission of San Juan bore the marks of high prosperity at a former period, and had a good pear-orchard just under the plateau where stood the church . . .

Spirit of the rancho years.

(The Century Illustrated)

Other reports say that almost all in that period slept on the ground, which had been pounded with mallets until quite hard and flat.

It is also said that many had *bailes* every night of the week.

There were multiple frictions in this period among the Mexican government, the church and the people. Some wanted to establish an independent

Spanish grist-mill used by early settlers. Wheat and corn were generally ground or pounded in the common hand stone mortar, but in larger settlements horsepower was used in turning or rolling one large stone upon another.

(Engraving in Elliott's history of the county)

Plow used by native Californians.

California, others were content to remain under Mexican rule, and still others favored joining the United States.

San Juan had its share of partisans, but this did not stop the pueblo from progressing as the largest community east of the Gabilans. Estimates of the population were not great —about six or seven hundred in the entire valley, with only one hundred and fifty in the village of San Juan, half of them Indians.

The rich farm land and the pleasant weather which encouraged both farming and cattle ranching attracted many settlers. The earliest came after receiving land grants from the Mexican government in the 1830s and early 1840s. During these years it was Mexican government policy to enlarge the population as protection from the Indians and to discourage foreign encroachment. To encourage this growth, the Mexican government began making land grants in the 1830s.

Soon after the final grant was made in 1846 by Governor Pio Pico, war broke out between Mexico and the United States. Final acceptance or rejection of the grants therefore fell to the United States, victor in the conflict.

It seems expedient to clarify this subject at this point. In the Treaty of Guadalupe Hidalgo, at the conclusion of the war, the United States agreed to respect the land grants which were issued and processed according to Mexican laws.

To process the grants the United States established a California Land Commission to examine and hold a hearing on each land grant. The decision could be appealed to the District Federal Court of California, and from there appealed to the United States Supreme Court, if either party wished to persist. The government was quite willing to issue a patent to the land if it was legally justified under both Mexican and United States laws.

Ten grants in the 1830s totaled 306,454 acres and seven in the 1840s totaled 152,118 acres. Of these 458,572 acres, an estimated 233,100 later became San Benito County. San Juan was the natural center for all these ranchos except in the southeast portion of the county, where there were a couple of small stores.

Six more grants were made, but one was to an Indian who never filed for legal title, and the other five were rejected by the California Land Commission for lack of evidence.

Two of the rejected claims had been granted by General José Castro when he was acting governor

The governors's carriage. Until the early 1840s there were no vehicles in California except ox carts. When Governor Micheltorena came to California in 1843, he brought as an ambulance a one-horse spring wagon. But in California he found no harness. Two mounted vaqueros were pressed into service. They lashed the shafts to their saddles and proceeded in regular California style.

(From drawing by Frederick Remington, in Pictorial History of California)

or prefect, as he was called while awaiting approval from Mexico of his appointment. It never came. Three other Castro grants were approved locally, but the U.S. Attorney appealed to the Supreme Court, which, after a delay of several years, granted the three titles to the land "by mandate, without an opinion." Obviously the court felt the grants were questionable but did not want to reject them after years of litigation.

Manuel Larios did not get title until August 8, 1870, nearly twenty years after filing. The others were settled a little sooner. The grantees had long been living on the land or might already have sold the grant; the court only confirmed existing circumstances.

General Castro

General Castro's home, c. 1940, built in the late 1830s. Castro also used it as his headquarters when he was general of the Northern Califonria Mexican army. He loaned and then sold it to the Breen family. It is now part of the state park.

There were some fraudulent claims in the state, but they were not numerous and only a handful of men were involved.

There are stories about many of the land grants, but this is a book about San Juan. For more details on land grants, the reader will find Marjorie Pierce's book, *East of the Gabilans,* an excellent source of information about the grants and the people who developed them.

One of the grants was just northeast of San Juan. The owner started what surely was the first manufacturing operation in the area.

José Maria Sanchez received the Rancho del Tequesquite from José Castro in 1835. Soon afterward, with Thomas O. Larkin, Sanchez began a commercial soap-making plant. It was located on the shores of Soap Lake—later San Felipe Lake—about five miles northeast of San Juan. The operation was closed in 1848 when everybody went off to the gold country.

The pueblo of San Juan, the name that appeared on early maps, was located in a strategic place to be involved and to benefit from the growth of the state. Its white population was small and by 1839 numbered only fifty persons.

José Tiburcio Castro was for many years the accepted leader of the community. He was also the manager of the mission properties after secularization but preferred to be called chief mayordomo. He would have liked for the pueblo to be known as San Juan de Castro, but the name never caught on.

Castro's management record was not outstanding. In 1836, under his stewardship, the mission lands had an income of $911 and expenses of $1,314, $312 of which was for goods and produce given to the Indians. As manager Castro received $262; $140 was paid to an assistant, Angel Castro, and $171 to Joaquin Rios.

It is noteworthy that after the report of 1836 there are no reports by the mayordomo. Neither is there any mention of the benefits given to Father Anzar, who dutifully remained at this post as parish priest. In 1844 Father Anzar held the post of Father Presidente of Zacatecan Franciscans in California.

The governor's office seemed to have a revolving door following Governor Echeandia's five and a half years in office, which ended in January 1831. Eight men held the office between then and November 1836, when Juan B. Alvarado became governor. He held the office until December 1842.

Alvarado, a close friend of General José Castro, established his headquarters in San Juan but moved to Monterey when he was appointed governor.

Two visitors to San Juan in the early 1840s found the mission and pueblo in very poor condition.

This sketch of the mission and plaza is dated 1842. The figures appear to be in religious processionals, possibly as part of a fiesta. In the rancho days the plaza was used for races, riding skills and rodeos, which those on the sidelines are waiting to participate in.

A French traveler and writer, Eugene de Mofras, found "now all lying in waste. The neophytes are dispersed. The small number of them that still hang around, barely a hundred, are reduced to a state of extreme misery."

Father Gonzalez, the bishop's secretary, was almost as distressed, as only the orchards were left and did not warrant fencing and maintenance. He reported, "I have exhorted my brethren to be patient, and to provide for their sustenance . . . from alms and other honorable receipts."

Five months after Manuel Micheltorena succeeded Alvarado as governor, he signed an order restoring the missions to the care of the Franciscans. They would have control of the churches, dwellings, priests, servants, gardens, vineyards, orchards and cemeteries. Some missions had remnants of the herds, some had a few implements. A small number of Indians remained in the San Juan area.

With some of the poorer lands which had not been granted to land-hungry citizens, it was hoped that the missionaries could again develop a profitable operation for their "children" and regain their former status. Alas, the hopes were short-lived.

The plot for the destruction of Micheltorena's program began in San Juan under the leadership of General José Castro and former Governor Alvarado. They conspired to drive Micheltorena out of the country. The governor learned of their plans and hired a party of riflemen under Captain Sutter.

Micheltorena and his men followed the conspirators as far south as Los Angeles, where for some reason Sutter and his men deserted Micheltorena. The governor realized that he could not depend on his Mexican troops, so he offered to resign and return to Mexico. His resignation was accepted on February

A drawing of a bullfight on the Plaza c.1850. All participants were local men.

24, 1845. He returned to Monterey, and he and his wife sailed for San Blas within a month.

Almost immediately Pio Pico announced that the territorial assembly had named him governor. He attacked the mission system without delay and set about establishing pueblos on mission property. Other mission property would be sold to pay debts, not to help the Indians or the church.

Pio Pico's provisional appointment was soon confirmed by Mexican authority, and he proceeded to

Captain John C. Fremont

Captain John C. Fremont is credited with encouraging a group of American settlers to seize the town of Sonoma from the Mexican army in the spring of 1846. As they did not represent the United States, they could not raise the stars and stripes and therefore constructed a new flag. The base of the flag was new white cotton cloth, a red strip taken from a red flannel petticoat worn across the plains was sewed along the bottom. Because of the presence of the bear, it was known as the Bear Flag. They raised the new Bear Flag of California on June 14, 1846, but they had overemphasized the danger of an attack by Mexican forces. Within a month the stars and stripes were flying over the state.

(Pictorial History of California)

press his plans to sell or grant mission property to individuals. In 1845 all mission property was put on sale, except the mission chapel, the curate's home and the land immediately around it. Whatever land sales were made were superseded by legal action in 1853.

By the mid-1840s San Juan (the official name of the town until 1905) had a population of approximately one hundred and fifty, about half white and half Indian.

San Juan might have been a tranquil town in the mid-forties if it had not been for a man named Brevet Captain John Charles Fremont of the United States Topographical Engineers. In 1845, Fremont was in the Oregon Territory exploring new routes for the growing number of settlers who were mov-

This house, built in 1835, was the first frame building erected by Americans in California. Located on Second Street opposite the mission, it served as the Ox Cart Tavern and trading post until 1857 when it was enlarged to be a residence. George W. Crane, an attorney and former assemblyman, resided here with his wife Maria Encarnacion. It has since been known as the Crane House. Crane died in 1868, a victim of the small pox epidemic. His wife continued to live in the house until her death in 1894.

FREMONT RAISED THE FIRST AMERICAN FLAG

The soil of San Benito county claims the honor of having sustained the first American flag of conquest ever unfurled to a California "breeze." General Fremont having floated the U.S. flag on the Gabilan Peak in March 1846.

This statement has often been challenged as not being a historical fact. But I believe a careful examination of the facts connected with the conquest and possession of California by the United States will justify the assertion.

It is to borne in mind, however, that the taking of Monterey, and the raising of the American flag over that town by Commodore Jones of the U.S. Navy, on October 19, 1842, does not enter into account; inasmuch as the action of the commodore was premature and in no sense a justifiable taking, because his government was on friendly terms with Mexico. And, moreover, the United States authorities repudiated the act; and the commodore himself, on the following day, hauled down the Stars and Stripes and saluted the Mexican flag, which he caused to be run up in its place while he in person made full and ample apologies to the then Governor of California, Micheltorena.

—The San Benito Advance of January 29, 1881

ing west. He had a detachment of sixty-two technicians and specialists, but all were armed, and Fremont had secret orders about his possible role in California.

In October 1845 officials in Washington gave secret orders to Marine Lieutenant Archibald Gillespie to deliver in California to the U.S. ambassador, to American admirals and generals, and to Fremont. Gillespie made good time—six months coming by way of Mexico and the Sandwich Islands (Hawaii). He arrived in Monterey with his memorized orders on April 17, 1846, three months before the written orders came around the Horn.

There are many versions of Fremont's activities in the San Juan area. We have found the author of the 1882 history of San Benito County to be quite accurate. Identified only as "an old timer," the author had a special advantage. He lived in San Juan and had personally met General Castro. He also had the benefit of informants who had firsthand knowledge of the episode. The following is an epitomized reprint of his account of the historic event:

Fremont brought his men back to Captain Johann (*sic*) Sutter's place on the American River. They arrived in December 1845 and soon went south into the San Joaquin Valley. With a growing threat of war, Mexican authorities did not like to have many North Americans in California. Near the end of January 1846, Fremont left his men in the valley and went to San Juan Bautista to ask Commanding General José Castro for permission to winter in the interior before returning to Oregon. General Castro had earlier told Fremont that he was free to go where he wanted.

Later, Castro reflected that the young captain was in command of a company of hated Americanos, and being doubtless advised by the home government that the United States was nibbling at California, as it had already taken a large mouthful of Mexican territory, by fomenting the trouble that led to the loss of Texas, he countermanded the permission. He sent a peremptory order to Fremont to quit the country or bear the consequences, which, it was hinted, would be death.

Captain Fremont's instructions were, in part, not to precipitate any difficulties with the Mexican authorities in California, and in no case to be the aggressor. Here, then, was a serious difficulty; acting on the permission previously given, to go where he pleased, he had led his company to the vicinity of San Juan, and was remounting his men by buying or exchanging for horses with the natives. He was also laying in a supply of dried beef, which he found no difficulty in purchasing at San Juan.

Naturally, he was somewhat alarmed, and greatly incensed by the general's curt message. He considered that he was justified in treating Castro's conduct as a breach of faith, and so he returned an answer as defiant as the message, to the effect that "he would go when he got ready."

As a soldier, he feared nothing; but as a diplomat, he was not sure that he was not transcending his orders. He was, doubtless, well advised that it was a foregone conclusion that California was to be acquired either by treaty, purchase or conquest; but his part in the game was not "to spring the mine."

All the time he was hopeful that General Castro would be satisfied with the promulgation of the order, and would make no attempt to enforce it. But he was disappointed. The general received the defiant answer as an act of hostility; he sent messengers over the country bearing the peculiarly Mexican proclamation that the soil of California was being desecrated by the Americanos del Norte, and appealing to his countrymen to take horse and arms (the Californians

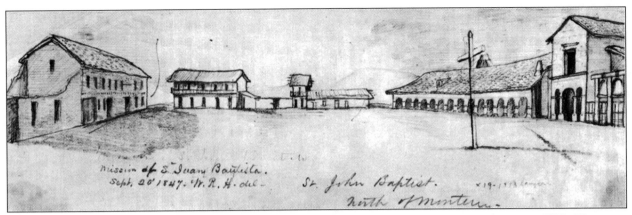

Mission of S. Juan Bautista.
Sept. 20 1847. W. R. H. del—

St. John Baptist.   ×19·1853 Langley
north of Monterey.

This is what the United States acquired under the peace terms with Mexico. Surveyor and engineer W. R. Hutton, on September 20, 1847, made this sketch of the plaza and surrounding buildings. He wrote that the beef was good, but he complained of the fleas. His companions, like other visitors of the era, didn't "like the fleas much." Hutton retreated from his bed and slept on straw in a shack.

always fought on horseback) and annihilate the invaders.

This appeal met a ready response. Soon a cavalry squadron of five or six hundred men rendezvoused on the Salinas plains near Natividad.

Matters began to look serious, and Captain Fremont concluded to retire, at his leisure, however, but to leave nothing undone to make a defense if attacked. He accordingly abandoned the Mission of San Juan, and led his company, with their horses, provisions and munitions of war, up the steep acclivities leading to the Gabilan Mountains which overlook the towns of Hollister and San Juan. He camped, erected a flag-staff, unfurled the Stars and Stripes, and calmly awaited the attack.

But the attack was not delivered; Castro maneuvered his command, deployed his skirmishers, and exhibited a variety of "high fantastic military tricks" at the foot of the Gabilan Mountains. He issued hourly proclamations and bulletins relating to the ruthless invaders, and fixing the exact hour at which he would give the command to charge (due notice of which was always imparted to the little band behind their improvised rampart on the hill). But as often as the command to charge was given, the courage of the soldiers was overcome by more pressing duties or preparations.

Finding that something more than "pomp and circumstance of war" was necessary to dislodge the enemy, but having no other resources at his command, the general concluded to withdraw his forces. But being somewhat careful of his reputation as a military man, he issued another bulletin, ostensibly to Fremont, but really to his own command.

This bulletin was to the effect that the general and his soldiers were anxious to fight, and to shed their blood, but that they were not disposed to climb the mountains to do so. The bulletin concluded with the challenge: *"Salganse al plan, yo no soy cierbo"* (come down the plain, I am not an elk), meaning that it was not convenient for him to follow his enemy to the mountain retreat.

The spot where Captain Fremont halted his company and raised the flag is on the San Benito side of the division line between Monterey and San Benito counties and the prominent peak which rises just above the spot is today [1882] better known as Fremont's Peak than as the Gabilan Peak, as it was called by the Californians.

It is not necessary to follow the subject further except for the purpose of getting Fremont out of his unpleasant predicament. Finding that Castro had dismissed his men to San Juan and Monterey, possibly on furlough to recuperate after the arduous campaign, and being satisfied that the "battle" would not be fought, Fremont determined to retire toward the Oregon line, there to await further developments. With this end in view, he struck camp and leisurely followed the summit of the Gabilan Range, at no point descending to the valleys, until he reached the Cholon, now known as Bear Valley, in southern San Benito County. From thence he struck to the north, the Big Panoche Valley to San Joaquin, where he was tarrying when the "stirring news" that he had been expecting reached him, that the United States had declared war against Mexico, and he was to seize and hold California, with all the resources at his command.

So ended the military confrontation of Mexican and American forces in San Juan in the spring of 1846.

Both Castro and Fremont played active roles in the war between Mexico and the United States that followed, but we must limit war news to that which relates to San Juan.

Fremont returned to San Juan sooner than expected. In the fall of 1846 he received orders to bring his volunteer units to Southern California where U.S. forces were experiencing resistance from the Mexican army. He chose San Juan as his staging area, and by November he had 495 mounted riflemen and forty-one artillerymen organized into ten companies. Those must have been exciting days for the little town.

On November 29 the force left San Juan and went south almost to Santa Barbara. Fremont befriended a landowner who warned him that Mexican forces were prepared to trap Fremont and his men in the narrow, rocky passes on the El Camino Real and wipe them out from above with boulders and bullets from well-protected positions. He took the man's advice and detoured through the mountains where a hundred horses were lost on the rough terrain.

During the weeks required for the trip the United States troop from San Diego had suppressed the Mexicans but had not completed a peace treaty. Fremont's command reached the San Fernando area, where they encountered remnants of forces under Andrés Pico. Fremont entered into the Treaty of Cahuenga, terms of which were later accepted by both sides to end the war in California.

And it all began in San Juan, where Fremont had the added pleasure of raising the American flag over the mission in General Castro's home town after the hostilities were over.

LAND GRANTS IN SAN BENITO COUNTY

Year	Rancho Name	Acreage	Grantee	Patented by
1835	Los Aromitos y Agua Caliente	8,659	Lucian M. Anzar	Frederick A. McDougal
1833	Ausaymas or Canada de Osos	35,504	Francisco P. Pacheco	Same
1835	Llano del Tequesquite	16,016	José M. Sanchez	Vicente Sanchez
1839	Rincón del Pájaro	33	Mariano Castro	Refugio Castro
1839	San Justo	34,615	José Castro	Francisco P. Pacheco
1836	San Joaquín or Rosa Morada	7,424	Cruz Gutierrez	Same
1839	Santa Ana y Quién Sabe	48,822	Marío Larios	Marío Larios y Juan Anzar
1833	San Ysidro (portion in county)	164	Quentín Ortega	Same
1839	Larios Tract near San Juan Bautista	4,493	Manuel Larios	Same
1835	Rancho de los Vergeles	150,720	José J. Gomez	James Stokes
1840	Bolsa de San Felipe	6,795	Francisco P. Pacheco	Same
1842	Los Carneros	1,629	Mario Antonio Larios	Frederick A. McDougal
1843	Cienega del Gabilan	48,780	Antonio Cháves	Jesse D. Carr
1842	Cienega de los Paicines	8,918	Angel Castro	Same
1842	Lomérios Muertos	6,659	José A. Castro	Vicente Sanchez
1844	Real de los Aguilas	31,052	Francisco Arias	Frederick A. McDougal
1846	San Lorenzo	48,285	Rafael Sanchez	Same

It was not until February 2, 1848, that the treaty of peace between the United States and Mexico was signed at Guadalupe Hidalgo. Lands in what was later to become San Benito County were mostly in the hands of the Mexicans. They had received sixteen land grants with an estimated total of 233,100 acres. Adjusted for some that extended over the county boundary, this represented about one-quarter of the county.

The United States government made every effort to recognize every grant that conformed to Mexican laws. Grantees often sold the land grant while title was being established. This resulted in the patent being issued to a person other than the grantee.

A GROWING TOWN

fter fifteen years of secularization the mission was greatly changed from the busy center of the productive years. Most of the buildings not connected to the church were roofless in 1850 and soon were piles of rubble.

The church had been improved and by then had pews, and the altars were well decorated. The buildings adjacent to the church, which had been used as habitations and storehouses, were better constructed than the outlying buildings, and some were rented as living quarters. The others were used by the resident clergy.

In 1849, a foreign visitor wrote of his visit to the mission:

Our party rode up to the archway of double width. Received by Don Juan Anzar and his brother, the padre.

Padre Anzar wore coarse gray habit of the Franciscan and a handkerchief tied around his head. About fifty years of age, of good figure, face and features. What anywhere would be called a fine looking man, with an expression of cheerfulness and good nature.

They received us with great urbanity and cordiality. Conducted us to the *sala*—a long room furnished in usual manner—chairs, settees, prints and looking glasses. Everything scrupulously clean and neat. Upon brackets against the walls stood vases of fine roses.

In 1846 Governor Pio Pico made an effort to give the mission properties to Ollivier Deleiseques in consideration of supplies he furnished the government in Monterey. The district court rejected the claim in 1855 as being unauthorized.

A special claim was filed February 19, 1853, by the Catholic church through J. S. Alemany, archbishop of Monterey. It was for three parcels total-

ing 55,231 acres. Included were the orchard, the vineyard and "the church and buildings adjoining it, built so as to form the sides of the quadrangle, enclosed on the other parts with an adobe wall. . . . Also, the premises known as the Garden of the Mission . . . and the cemetery.

The claim was finally patented after several hearings and a detailed survey by J. W. Mandeville, United States surveyor general for California. It was signed by President James Buchanan, November 19, 1859.

Spanish names still dominated the farm and business life of San Juan in 1850, but many people were arriving from the East or directly from European countries other than Spain. They found not only a town and fertile land, but also a hunter's paradise. Isaac Mylar, who arrived in town in the early 1850s, wrote, "Game in the San Juan Valley . . . was plentiful. There were geese, ducks, quail by the millions, cotton-tail rabbits and the hills were full of deer."

Construction in San Juan and the surrounding towns in the 1850s soon prompted the building of a sawmill on Pescadero Creek a few miles northwest of town. New names operated it—Silas Twitchell and then William Stingley. In addition to building supplies for the town, smaller items were exported from the area in the form of shakes, pickets, shingles and posts.

If not the first, at least the most famous new name in the area arrived in February 1848, when Patrick Breen and family settled in San Juan.

The Breens had left their home in Iowa two years earlier. They were in a pre-Gold Rush wagon train of more than two hundred families. At Salt Lake they joined a small group under the leadership of George and Jacob Donner to take a "short cut" over the mountains. The story of the Donner Party's ordeals the delays, being snowbound, the

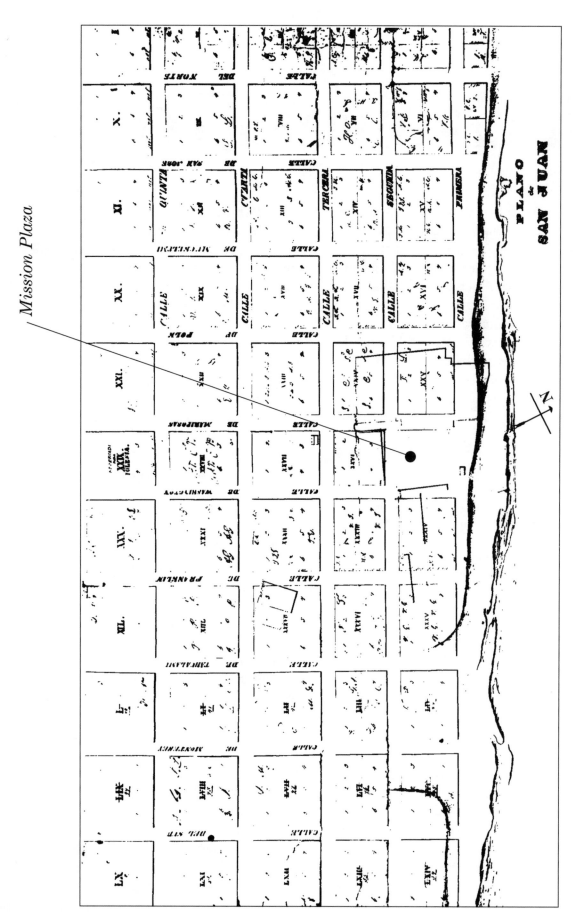

The "Plano de San Juan" drawn by Herman Ehrenberg in 1849 was discovered by the authors of a report to the California State Park Commission in 1931. They wrote, "This is not only one of the earliest, but one of the most complete and accurate plans of San Juan it has been our fortune to find." It was noted that the plan indicated that the plaza was originally intended to be a fore-court or cloister of the mission. Members of the Zanetta and Anzar family concurred, and early photos show a fence some distance from the church. Contrary to normal practice, the top of this map is to the South.

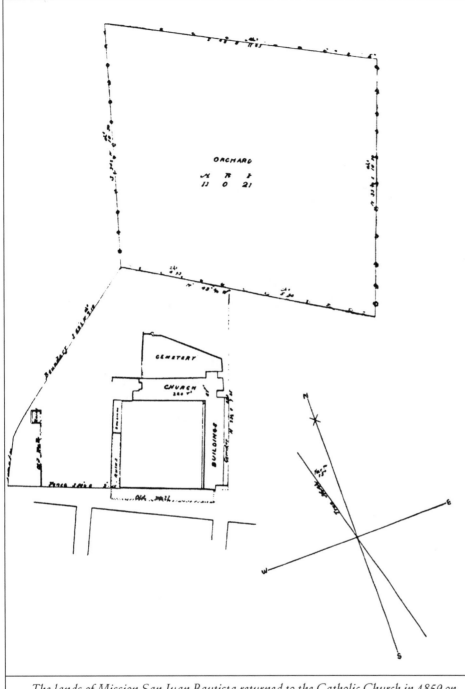

The lands of Mission San Juan Bautista returned to the Catholic Church in 1859 on a claim filed in 1853.

be patented to Refugio Castro, after thirty years of litigation, Breen's title was validated

The Gold Rush resulted in a bit of a rush in San Juan as people swarmed up the Camino Real on their way to the mines. There were no hotels in San Juan, and Patrick and Margaret Breen rose to the occasion by offering their home to travelers.

The house was called the United States Tavern Inn, and variations of that name, and won praise from a few who later wrote about their visits there. They wrote especially of Margaret Breen, who was regarded as one of the heroines of the Donner Party. How long the Breen home was operated as a sort of hotel is uncertain; nobody kept track of that information.

In 1848 the oldest Breen son, John, responded to the Gold Rush by joining it. He enjoyed success at Mormon Bar and the following year returned with a reported $12,000 in gold dust.

John and his six siblings remained in San Benito County and they and their descendants have served in public office and participated in major activities over a period of nearly a century and a half.

Edward Smith was named postmaster when San Juan was granted a post office on July 28, 1851. There were only sixty-one post offices in the state at that time. It has generally been reported that prior to the opening of San Juan's post office, people received their mail through Gilroy. Records show that Gilroy did not have a post office until almost four months later, October 21, 1851. An explanation

deaths and the rescue of the survivors—has been told in several books.

When the family arrived in 1848, General Castro let them live in his house on the square. He later "sold" the house to the Breens, although he had not received title to it. When he was acting governor he granted that lot and two other small town lots to Mariano Castro. It was March 1885 before the United States Supreme Court ordered the land to

The barren plaza in this photo of the late fifties or early sixties reflects the written description of the mission. A low fence can barely be seen along the front.

might be that the mail may have come to Gilroy out of another post office and was picked up by someone and brought to San Juan.

In 1853 Postmaster Smith died, and Patrick Breen was named to replace him, but there was a problem. Patrick did not want the job, but his oldest son, John, did. Rather than disturbing postal officials in Washington with such details, Patrick appointed John assistant postmaster, and John conducted all post office business for several years.

The post office was named San Juan. It was not until fifty-four years later, on November 16, 1905, that it was changed to San Juan Bautista. The town was sometimes called San Juan South to distinguish it from San Juan North, a mining town near Grass Valley in northern California. Later there were vexing delays when mail was sent to the larger and better-known San Juan Capistrano, but in this century San Juan Bautista is firmly established in both name and location.

In the early years after the Gold Rush and the establishment of California as a state in the Union, many individuals took an active part in building San Juan. It is unfortunate that we cannot present a complete honor roll, but space is limited, as is the source of names of all the pioneers who came, saw, and stayed.

Many of the early arrivals were farmers and ranchers, who found the soils and rangelands among the best. San Juan became the center for the artisans and businessmen who served them. Other businessmen and professionals naturally stayed to serve the entire population of the area.

The following list has been compiled from a number of sources:

William Prescott, Mr. Edmundson, R. W. Canfield, Silas Twitchell, J. B. McKee, F. A. McDougal, J. D. Carr, and James Stokes.

One of the early doctors was C. G. Cargill, who also owned a drugstore which later added the post office and Wells Fargo & Company express. In the 1880s the telephone office was located there. Dr. Cargill also served three terms as assemblyman from the area, the only Republican to hold the position prior to 1900.

Blacksmiths: John Hunt, E. W. Bowman, Clarence Bowman, J. R. Allen.

Wheelwright: William Bowman.

Painters: Walter Bowman, John Nagle.

Sheriff: William Burnett.

Tinsmith: John Anderson.

Stage owners: William Burnett, Mark Regan.

Brewery owner: J. G. (Jake) Beuttler.

Hotel proprietors: Angelo Zanetta and A. Camours, the Plaza; John Geaster (builder in 1858) and George Pullen, the National; Angelo Zanetta, the Sebastopol (before the Plaza).

Shoe store proprietors: J. Brietbarth, H. Beger.

Gunsmith and locksmith: S. Durin.

General merchandise storekeepers: James Mahon, Daniel Harris, Mr. Pratalongo, Felipe Gardella.

Wine sellers: V. Gerbet (or Jerbet), Theophile Vache.

Saddle and harness shopkeeper: James Stanley.

Baker: Jean Lacoste.

Restaurateur: C. Quersin.

Grist mill proprietor: Bill and Nels Williamson, mill on the river; unknown, mill on south side of Fourth Street in the early 1860s.

Patrick and Margaret Breen

Patrick Breen of the Donner Party tragedy. He became San Juan Bautista's postmaster in 1853.

Margaret Breen. She was credited with getting the family through the horror in the snow.

Saloon keepers: Luis Raggio, Sr. Fred Kemp, Vic McGarvey.

Then there were the Breens, all nine of them, the Bixbys, the Flints and the Anzars.

California's population increased rapidly in the early 1850s, resulting in a good deal more travel on El Camino Real. As in earlier years, almost every traveler going north or south passed through San Juan. Many stages stopped over for the night, and hotels were quickly built or enlarged.

Angelo Zanetta, who had run the Sebastopol Hotel on Third Street, took over the Plaza Hotel on the square. He rebuilt the first floor, retaining the adobe walls, and added a second floor built of wood and plaster.

The remodeled Plaza was opened with a grand fiesta in 1856 and was considered second to none in California. Zanetta became noted all over the state for the fine food he served at the hotel. It was headquarters for traders of sheep, cattle, horses and hogs, a free spending lot that any hotel or town would welcome.

Over on Third Street new businesses were being built after the remains of the auxiliary mission buildings had been cleared away. Two stories are told about discoveries as the work along the street progressed. One is that two large pails of coins were found by a construction foreman. The other, as told in the 1880s, was that a road master found a roll of sixty silver Spanish coins bearing a date of the early eighteenth century. Both were apparently hidden in a building or buried. Which is true? Both? Neither? A definitive answer at this late date is very unlikely.

By 1856 the town had four general merchandise stores, and Third Street was lined with saloons and businesses, including a blacksmith and wheelwright, gunsmith, livery stable, bakery, jewelry store, horseshoer and the Sebastopol Hotel.

The names of the owners of these general merchandise firms offer good evidence of the cosmopolitan nature of this village: James McMahon, Irish; Daniel Harris, English; Felipe Gardella, Italian; and Mr. Pratalongo, French.

Another example of the changing makeup of the town was the "regular" group of cribbage players in the mission on most winter nights. The regulars were merchant Daniel Harris, his mother, Dr. McDougal, and Father Mora. The priest later became a bishop and then retired to Spain.

Kemp's Saloon — Circa 1860

of the missioh. This also was the date of the grand reopening of the Plaza Hotel in 1856.

The event was well remembered by Isaac Mylar, as were many more events in the next seventy years. Let him tell you about this fiesta, much of which was typical of the subsequent fiestas in good years in San Juan:

From the ranchos, far and near, came the Dons with their families. To me, a boy of eight years, it was a great sight. A band was engaged and played on the veranda of the hotel for the delectation of the populace. The veranda was crowded with señoritas and women of other nationalities, all in gay attire.

After attending Mass in the morning at the old mission, which fronts the plaza, the fun would commence.

The gay caballeros, gaudily attired and riding finely comparisoned horses, would display their horsemanship in many ways. Backing up some distance, they would ride on the plaza at full speed and pick up money, handkerchiefs, and even pluck a chicken's head from its body—the chicken being buried in the ground with only its head above the surface.

In order to make the celebration as noisy and impressive as possible the old cannon was raised from the ground and placed on the back part of a wagon. This cannon was fired at regular intervals all day and away into the night, and, of course, this bombardment was a great attraction for us youngsters.

Here and there could be seen, on these occasions, a Don attired in a *serape* (a finely made blanket with a hole in the center through which the head of the wearer was thrust). Some of these cloaks (serapes) were very valuable. They were made of the finest materials, and had silk worked into them as

The Harris family lived in the row of rooms extending to Second Street from the mission. Their rooms were next to the priest, and other people lived in rooms closer to the street.

In San Juan reference to "the fiesta" always has meant the big event on or about June 24, the feast day of Saint John the Baptist and the founding day

In 1858 another hotel was built in the growing town. The National Hotel of John Geaster was located at the corner of Second and San Jose streets. It included a bar and a large room on the second floor for meetings, dances, and shows by schools, local or traveling troupes. It later added a restaurant. It was used until torn down in the 1930s.

well as being orna-
mented in various
ways. They were rated
highly and com-
manded a big price.

The Mexicans
were given to wearing
broad-brimmed hats,
most of which came
from Chile and
Mexico.

The third and last
day was always
marked by the bull-
fighting. The climax
of the program was a
grand bull-and-bear
fight. In those days
the vaqueros would
arrange to go over to
the Quien Sabe
Rancho, now [1920s]
owned by the D. E.
Laveaga family, and
there the vaqueros
would capture a griz-
zly bear for the cel-

The Sebastopol Hotel was an early hotel, early enough to be in this sketch of 1853 by Henry Miller. It is the building with a cupola to the extreme left. The mission is to the right. The artist took artistic liberty with the locations of buildings and/or hills.

ebration. The grizzlies in those days used to
come down onto the plains to feed, and the
San Juan boys would take over a *carreta*. They

would lasso the bear and securely tie him and
would bring him back in the carreta to San
Juan where he would be confined until wanted
on the day of the cel-
ebration.

The bulls were
kept in a pen con-
nected with the main
corral, and the bear
that was to mix things
with the bull, was
generally kept away
some distance from
the plaza in a building
selected for that pur-
pose. The bear was in
a cage which was kept
on the carreta, and
when the time arrived
for the combat to be-
gin the carreta was
drawn into the corral,
the bear safely tied to
a stake in the ground,
and the cage and
carreta taken away.

The Sebastopol Hotel continued operation until 1891, when it burned. This photo was dated two years before that. The French Restaurant advertised on the building was operated by Fenclon Filicheau.

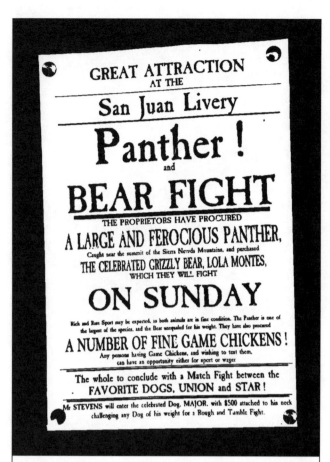

A matching of animals like this was popular in early California. This poster was created by a Park volunteer to depict what may have been.

A carretta was the universal form of conveyance in the early days of California

as many as 5,000 people attend one of these fiestas. They came from all directions, far and near. Where they slept or how they got food to eat, I do not know and I often wondered if providence sent ravens to feed them.

When a boy, I was sitting on a fence watching the proceedings at one of these festivals, and witnessed a premature explosion of the cannon which tore off Lon Woodworth's arm below the elbow.

The fiestas continued through the years but within ten years the bull-and-bear fights were dis-

$50.00
REWARD

The Above Reward will be paid to the Man who cannot find the
Faro Game
Which is now running in the
PLAZA HOTEL

First Chip FREE

Gambling was popular in the early days. This is a modern composite of how Faro might have been marketed.

A large enclosure would be constructed on the plaza inside of which bull-fighting would be indulged in. The bullfights in those days were not marked by the brutality seen at the bullfights in Spain. The mission padres would not permit any brutality. The sport was largely in the shape of feats of horsemanship pitted against the onrushes of the bull and the agility of the matadors to get out of the way of the enraged animal's onslaught.

On the day of the bear fight, the bear would be attached to a pole in the center of the enclosure. He would have a run of about twenty feet around the pole to which he was attached by a strong *riata*. The bull was similarly tethered by one foot. Invariably, the bear would be killed inasmuch as he would stand on his hind feet to receive the oncoming bull who would, with so fair a target before him, generally rip the bear open after a few thrusts. The bull usually escaped with a few scratches, although I have seen some of the bulls so badly mangled that they had to be killed. I have seen

continued. Bullfights did not last much longer, and rodeo-type events became the popular attraction for the fiestas.

The Catholic church has always celebrated the anniversary of the mission, but many times community support has waned due to depressed econom-

WILL BE EXHIBITED
FOR ONE DAY ONLY!

AT THE PLAZA HOTEL
THIS DAY FROM 9 A.M., UNTIL 6 P.M.

THE HEAD
Of the renowned Bandit!

JOAQUIN MURIETA

AND THE
HAND OF THREE FINGERED JACK!
THE NOTORIOUS ROBBER AND MURDERER.

"JOAQUIN" and "THREE FINGERED JACK" were captured by the State Rangers, under the command of Capt. Harry Love, at the Arroyo Cantina, July 24th. No reasonable doubt can be entertained in regaurd to the identification of the head now on exhibition, as being that of the notorious robber, Joaquin Murieta, as it has been recognised by hundreds of persons who have formerly seen him.

This is a reproduction of a poster made by a Park volunteer for an interpretative event. The Plaza Hotel would have had to offer this attraction soon after opening. Joaquin Murieta was killed July 24, 1853, and his head was displayed for several months in San Francisco in 1854. Yes, many people identified Murieta, but there was probably an equal number who denied it was he.

ics or population. Some fiestas in the early part of this century were related to community progress and will be reported with the associated activities.

Although many of the early pioneers had little or no schooling, they knew the value of an education. Schools were soon organized, and in 1852 a school board was elected, but early classes were irregular. The board consisted of Patrick Breen, John Jordan and one other whose name was lost and never remembered.

The first classes were held in a private home donated by an unnamed owner. For most of the next six years the children attended schools in other homes, some of which required rent. There was just one teacher, and he sometimes did not get paid for the entire year because the board ran out of money. When that happened the students would have a longer than usual vacation period. The teacher sometimes set up a private school where students could pay tuition and complete their term.

The teachers were almost invariably men, most of whom were trained for other work for which there was no demand in the early Western societies. Often they were attorneys or ministers, and they were of varied ethnic backgrounds. Three early teachers remembered by Mylar were William B. Harris, who was a member of the Cherokee tribe, a Mr. Cooper, and the Rev. Azarih Martin.

By 1859 the board had arranged for construction of a small school at the west end of Third Street on Rocks Road near El Camino Real. In later years Alfred Harris estimated the size of the building to be twenty-nine by forty feet, divided into two rooms.

As they sat in school, students found the travelers passing on the "highway" most intriguing. A Mexican with his slow oxen pulling a squeaky-wheeled carreta might be followed by a stagecoach loaded with wealthy travelers from the big cities. Buggies, both personal and freight wagons, as well as lone horsemen would add further interest to their day aside from their lessons.

The school itself was primitive. The one chair was reserved for the teacher. Students sat on rough benches and used whatever desk they might have brought from home. The students were required to sweep out the building. Hygiene was something that no one knew anything about. It was a common practice for all students to drink water from the same cup dipped into a bucket of well water.

"And yet," Mylar wrote, "under the simple guidance of these educators, we learned the three R's and learned them well."

There is no doubt but that Samuel M. Shearer was considered the best teacher ever to teach at the school. Both Mylar and Harris speak highly of his ability, even though he expelled Harris. Shearer was principal for a short time and then moved to Salinas, where he became county superintendent of schools. After his retirement he wrote a series of articles about San Juan while editor of the *Index* newspaper.

The school board levied its first school tax in 1868 and built a new school near First Street. Mylar described it as "where the high school was later built," and Dorothy Flint, another pioneer and author of *Escarpment on the San Andreas*, identified it as "a location near the western end of the escarpment on which the mission was situated . . . "

By 1875 the San Juan school had grown to a three-teacher school, even though the district had been reduced in size when fourteen additional districts were formed in the county. The county then had 1,450 school-aged children, but less than half of them attended school.

When Dorothy Flint attended school in 1909 it was in a new stucco building, but it was still a three-teacher school.

The two-story high school remained at the same site until 1933, when it was joined with the Hollister Union High School District.

San Juan benefited from two developments in the mid-1850s, even though they occurred in the other end of the county. They deserve to be discussed because of their impact on San Juan and also because San Juan was the largest community east of the Gabilans for a hundred miles.

Theophilus Vache, born in France in 1814, arrived in Monterey County about twenty-five years later. In the interim he worked at his trade as a baker in three countries and six states of the United States.

After arriving in the area, he first engaged in dairying and sheep-raising. In 1854 he planted his first vineyard on his 320-acre farm at Paceines, eight miles south of where Hollister would later be located.

By the 1880s Vache had twenty-five varieties of grapes and was producing from ten to fifteen thousand gallons of wines per year. He also sold several kinds of table grapes.

To sell his wines Vache established a store in San Juan on the southeast corner of Third and Washington streets. The adobe building is still there and is part of the Jardines de San Juan Restaurant building.

As San Juan grew the hotels were happy to have good local wines to serve their guests. In 1883 Vache sold his ranch to William Palmtag of Hollister.

The second activity was farther from San Juan but of greater importance. In the eastern part of San Benito County cinnabar was found in large quantities. Cinnabar is a red mercuric sulfide ore from which mercury or quicksilver is derived. The heavy, silver-white metallic chemical elements are used in many ways but are of special value for wartime armaments.

The largest and most successful mine was the New Idria, which was of major importance to San Juan until 1870.

What are usually referred to as "responsible sources" say that New Idria was discovered and/or started operations in 1851, 1852, 1854 and 1856. The 1851 date is a likely discovery date, and 1854 has the most support for the date of the first mining operations. And then there is also a story that Indi-

San Juan Bautista Elementary School 1868

ans brought ore to the mission that was identified as quicksilver. Other mines were opened after that but were nowhere near the size of New Idria. They included the Monterey, San Benito, Picacho, Gonzales and the Fourth of July mines.

The importance of the mines to San Juan was the freight and travelers who journeyed through San Juan for more than fifteen years. The New Idria hired three hundred to five hundred men during that time, and practically all of their food and supplies passed through San Juan.

San Juan merchant Dan Harris supplied much of the needs of the mines. A dark cloud was cast over the Harris operations in the 1860s when William Healy Thompson, owner and superintendent of

New Idria

The operation of the New Idria Mine extended over several hundred acres. The town—it was really a company town—remained near the site of the original mine, which is marked but sealed. In later years there was a great deal of open-pit mining.

There were a great variety of buildings: company stores, dormitories for single men, and small houses for the married couples. A furnace is shown in the picture on the right. A tender had to stand there at all times, and the mercury contamination was deadly.

Three to five hundred men worked at the plant, most living in the dormitories. In 1905 early records and any pictures were lost when fire destroyed the company's headquarters in Boston.

the New Idria mine, became involved in an expensive court battle for the title to the mining property. His bill with Harris edged up to thirty thousand and then forty thousand dollars, but Harris continued deliveries. Everything came out all right as Thompson won title to the property.

The problem resulted from a claim by a William McGarrahan that the property was part of a land grant he owned. It came to trial in Fresno County, as the area was then still in that county. The story from Fresno was that the judgment was not handed down on the basis of facts. Mr. McGarrahan had imported a high priced attorney from San Francisco who did not know his judge.

Judge Chapman, before whom the case was tried, asked the attorney a question whose answer would disclose his political alignment. He answered honestly, disclosing an allegiance to the Union. But he realized that it was not a welcome answer. He pretended a bad coughing spell and rushed out for a drink to ease his throat. He asked the bartender the judge's politics, and the bartender replied, "Secession to hell and gone." The attorney returned to court, explained that his answer reflected his early beliefs but after great study of the question, etc., etc. . . . Whatever, Mr. McGarrahan lost and joy returned to the Harris store. Thompson gave Harris a beautiful silver centerpiece for his patience.

It has been impossible to compile an accurate history of the New Idria Quicksilver Mines Company because a fire in 1905 destroyed all records at the company's headquarters in Boston. Few records were retained in California.

Traffic through San Juan to New Idria dropped off quickly after the railroad was completed to Gilroy and then to Hollister. Dan Harris was one of the first to leave San Juan.

The mines continued to be one of the biggest producers of quicksilver for more than one hundred years. Production peaked during World War I with over six hundred employees. Troops were sent in, in 1918, to guard against sabotage because mercury was so important to the war effort.

Conditions remained primitive in many aspects, such as bandannas being the most common "mask" against poisonous mercury fumes. Early symptoms of salivating, shortness of breath, green gums and uncontrollable shakes were taken lightly, but death

usually followed from deposits of mercury in different organs of the body.

The mines remained in operation until June 1974, when the price of mercury that had sometimes reached $500 a flask dropped to $100 due to low-priced foreign competition. There was also need of better equipment to meet modern laws designed to protect the workers from mercury poisoning.

San Juan continued to grow and prosper in the 1860s but there were trying times, adversity and mistakes.

California received a drenching the winter of 1861-62 which is generally ranked as the worst the state has ever experienced. San Juan received its share.

The small stream that crossed the Alameda was always an awfully muddy place when it rained, so much so that wagons sometimes bogged down. In that wet winter, Mark Regan, a stagecoach operator, said the rains were so heavy that the ditch became a gorge.

Hillsides were washed away, there were many mud slides, and the valley was full of water. People could hardly leave their homes on many days, Regan said in a later interview.

This was true not only in the San Juan area but also throughout the state. Sheep and cattle were drowned, and it was weeks, sometimes months, before the ground could be worked for planting.

Teamsters were obliged sometimes to leave their wagons and bring their horses into town. Two teamsters were known to have been swept away between Sargent and town. Mylar also wrote that four of New Idria's six-horse teams mired near the later site of Hollister. They were finally freed by four yoke of oxen.

Later, a new, higher route was developed over the foothills southeast of town.

Records show an 1861-62 rainfall of 49.27 inches, or about twice the normal, but the damage resulted mostly from much of this total falling in a short period, which is not defined in the records.

The following year the weather returned to normal, but the winter of 1863-64 was dry—only 10.08 inches all year long.

With little spring rain there was limited grass for the cattle. Sheep apparently fared better because they could eat the grass shorter. Cattle were sold

THE HERITAGE OF SAN JUAN'S ADOBES

Buildings 150 years old are not numerous in the West, but San Juan Bautista has a fine collection of adobes. Most of them are still being used. The San Juan Bautista Mission and the three major buildings are of course the best known. There are more. The ones in these photos were built between 1833 and 1860.

The adobe barracks for soldiers was built next to General Castro's home. This is a sketch made in 1847. About six years later Angelo Zanetta acquired the building. He reinforced the adobe walls and added a wooden frame second floor which was opened as the Plaza Hotel with a grand fiesta in 1856.

The Pico-Boronda Adobe at 207 Fourth Street. It is shown here before (left) and after it was restored about 1933 by the Native Daughters of the Golden West.

The Juan de Anza Adobe was built in 1834 as the family residence. By 1850 it was being used commercially. This continued to 1933, when it housed the first antique store in San Juan. The same family has operated it for more than sixty years.

In the 1850s Theophile Vache needed a place to sell his wines. A two-story adobe had been built on the southeast corner of Third and Washington streets. Vache used it for about twenty years. It is now part of Jardines de San Juan.

Tuccoletta Hall, on the southwest corner of Third and Washington, was built by 1840. The lower floor was used as a bakery until 1880 and then as the merchandise store of the Lavagino family for fifty years. The upstairs hall was used for all types of meetings, many dances, and other events, including the first showing of a movie in San Juan.

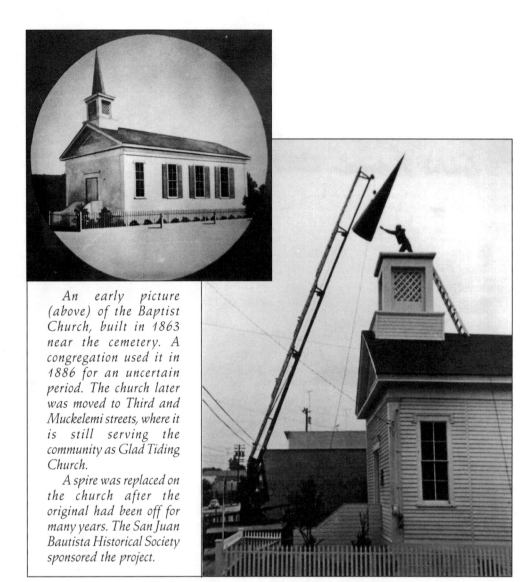

An early picture (above) of the Baptist Church, built in 1863 near the cemetery. A congregation used it in 1886 for an uncertain period. The church later was moved to Third and Muckelemi streets, where it is still serving the community as Glad Tiding Church.

A spire was replaced on the church after the original had been off for many years. The San Juan Bautista Historical Society sponsored the project.

for two and one-half dollars per head to people like cattle baron Henry Miller, who could use them at retail outlets in the Bay Area or put them on his land along San Joaquin Valley rivers.

Some cattle ranchers were obliged to drive their cattle to the slaughter house in Monterey. Those that survived the drive, often without water, were killed for their hides and horns. Some carcasses were sold for hog food. Hundreds of cattle died pitiful deaths as they struggled to find food or water.

In addition to the vagaries of the weather, or perhaps because of them, the 1860s saw a wave of spiritual arousal in San Juan. In 1864, San Juan witnessed the organization and construction of its first Protestant churches.

The Baptists erected a church on Monterey Street near the cemetery that year.

The first Methodist church was built at Second and Church streets. The Civil War created a schism in San Juan as it did in the rest of the country. The Methodist Church South retained the original building, and the Methodist Church North was erected on Church Street nearer the cemetery.

There were revival meetings in the churches, and outdoor revival meetings in tents were offered by local churches or by traveling ministers. Baptisms were often held in the river. But, as the population dropped the churches were deserted and moved or put to other use—all but the Baptist Church. It was moved to the southeast corner of Third and Muckelemi streets, where it still serves the community as the Glad Tidings Church. In 1974 the San Juan Bautista Historical Society sponsored a steeple restoration project for the church.

SITTING ON TOP OF THE WORLD

The Civil War being waged in the East and South during this period also touched San Juan. Many of the early settlers were from the South, and many felt an allegiance to the Southern cause and were usually called "Secessionists." All through the wet and dry weather the area had its concerns about the Civil War.

Shortly after the outbreak of the war the governor suggested that all California towns should organize home guard units for possible aid to the Union. The Unionists decided such action would probably provoke opposition and disunity in San Juan.

In the spring of 1862, Dorothy Flint wrote that when some of the family returned from the East "...the travelers had been aware of growing tension in San Juan. Secessionist sympathy—always proportionately much more prevalent there than in the City—was now such as to make the Flint and Bixby families, occupying the former Hollister house beside the pond on the San Justo, increasingly conscious of being part of a tragic estrangement even in their immediate vicinity. Consequently, while the women busied themselves with sewing the thirty-four stars and the wide stripes of an eighteen-foot flag that they hoped to raise first on the Fourth of July, the men had made certain that the flagpole on which it would be displayed high above the house would be transported through San Juan by night in order to avoid interception and possible bloodshed."

The situation might have continued on a peaceful basis if outlaws had not increased their activities in the area in 1863-64. Some of them bragged of secessionist connections and activities elsewhere in an effort to win acceptance in the community. Among them was a duo called the Mason-Henry gang. Mason's real name was Joe Mace, and he was said to be of Cherokee extraction. Henry's real name was

San Juan was growing in the 1860s but had no local police protection. This is not an original, but interpretative of the period. It was produced by a Park volunteer.

Thomas McCauly. He was wanted for a killing in Tuolumne before he teamed up with Mason.

Mason and Henry claimed to have been former Confederate soldiers. At times they tried to enlist supporters to join the Confederacy. "They were, in fact, freebooters of the most unmitigated kind, who took it into their heads to make war on the peaceable stockmen of the Panoche Valley, and the San Benito and Tres Pinos country," said the "Old Timer" in the 1881 *History of San Benito County.*

"They boasted of several atrocious murders; but their favorite pastime was to cut off and slit the ears of such persons as they disliked," he continued. Their crime record here and elsewhere was sadistic and cruel beyond belief.

It should be remembered that this was before San Benito County was established and there was no organized law enforcement unit. The closest law enforcement in the area was nearly a day's trip for the sheriff from Monterey. It is little wonder that the account continued: "The whole country south and east of San Juan was terrorized; the settlers and stockmen were compelled to seek refuge at San Juan, leaving their homes and flocks unprotected. Owing to this . . . and vague rumors of attempts to take California out of the Union . . . authorities determined to establish a military post . . . in San Juan."

Before the arrangements could be made for troops on the local "front," the first newspaper appeared in San Juan, on October 8, 1864. It was called

The Civil War visited San Juan, yet not a shot was fired in anger except at some suspected criminals. While California did her part in the Civil War, the troops stationed there had only time to kill, not an enemy. The Union Army troops stationed in San Juan Bautista were complimented for their morning formations and assistance in law enforcement.

This was reproduced from a contemporary print by Professor Owen C. Coy in his Pictorial History of California in 1925. Coy's legend to the print read: "Although far removed from the seat of the Civil War, California did her part in that national crisis. In enlistments in the United States Army she exceeded her quota, although her men were used very largely within her own borders relieving the regular army men for service in the south. Her gold mines furnished wealth when the national credit demanded all that could be produced. In the work of the Sanitary Commission, the forerunner of the Red Cross, California proved herself especially generous, contributing nearly a million and a quarter dollars, practically one-third of the total amount."

the *Monterey County Journal* or just *County Journal*, with San Juan as the town of publication. B. B. Barker was publisher and proprietor of the weekly, which would be published every Saturday morning.

It was not a coincidence that the *Monterey County Journal* was established when it was. The first issue was printed just before the Union Army

detachment was moved to San Juan, and less than a month before the presidential election.

In Vol. 1, No. 2, in his message "To The Public," Mr. Barker said he was "unexpectedly called upon to assume the proprietorship and publication of this paper . . . " He continued, saying that the politics of the paper would be Democratic (pro-Confederate or Secessionist in those days) and it would urge the election of George B. McClellan and the defeat of Abraham Lincoln.

Barker's weapons would be words to soften the enthusiasm of the Union troops being sent to San Juan. The word most often used was "peace." By late 1864 everyone wanted peace after four long years of war, and the newspaper's role was to win community support as well as some friendly consideration from the troops for the South.

Of course, by this time the war was going against the South, and Barker was obliged to report that early elections in the East were being won by President Lincoln. The *Journal*'s favorite campaign theme was, *"Mr. Lincoln will not make peace unless the South abandons slavery."* (italics ours)

The single edition of the *County Journal* located thus far was quite professional but it apparently failed to arouse contemporary writers such as Miss Flint and Mylar, neither of whom so much as mentioned it. Nor is it mentioned in the Elliot & Moore 1881 history of the county. Whether the newspaper continued publication beyond Vol. 1, No. 2 is not known.

MONTEREY COUNTY JOURNAL.

VOL. I. SAN JUAN, MONTEREY COUNTY, CAL., SATURDAY, OCTOBER 15, 1864. NO. 2.

COUNTY JOURNAL.

PUBLISHED EVERY SATURDAY MORNING.

B. B. BARKER,..... Proprietor.

TERMS.—One Year, $5; Six Months, $3.

ADVERTISEMENTS—First insertion of one square, Ten Lines or less, $2; each subsequent insertion $1 per square. Liberal deduction to Quarterly or Yearly Advertisers. Gold Coin in payment.

OFFICE—In Mission Building, Northwest corner Plaza, San Juan, Monterey County, California.

OUR AGENTS.

The following gentlemen will receive Subscriptions and Advertisements for this paper:

Thomas Boyce,..................San Francisco.
A. Waltrufel,..................San Jose.
P. B. Tully,..................Gilroy.
R. H. Brotherton,..(at Drug Store)...San Juan
Frank Johnson,..................Natividad.
James Bardin,..................Salinas.
James L. Seffole,..................Monterey City.
Chas. O'Neil,..................Watsonville.
A. Shearer,..................Pajaro.
Henry Rice,..................Santa Cruz.
John Daubenbiss..................Soquel.
Dr. Russell,..................Visalia.
R. R. Harris,..................San Luis Obispo.
E. Headley,..................Los Angeles.

PROFESSIONAL AND BUSINESS CARDS.

CARDS Published on this page at Five Dollars per Quarter (Ten lines or Less).

F. & A. M.

TEXAS LODGE, NO. 46, Meets at the Lodge Room, San Juan, every second Saturday Evening in each month. Visiting brethren in good standing are invited to be present.

GEO. W. CRANE,

ATTORNEY AT LAW—OFFICE, SAN JUAN, Monterey County, Cal. 1tf

JAMES F. BREEN.

ATTORNEY AT LAW—Office, San Juan, Monterey County, Cal. 1tf

SAMUEL F. GEIL.

ATTORNEY AT LAW—Office, Monterey City. District Attorney for Monterey Co. 1tf

P. K. WOODSIDE,

ATTORNEY AT LAW—Office, Monterey City, Cal. 1tf

JAS. W. THRIFT,

ATTORNEY AT LAW—Office, Pajaro Street, opposite Nebraska Hotel, Watsonville, Cal.

JULIUS LEE,

ATTORNEY AND COUNSELLOR AT LAW. Office, on Pajaro Street, Watsonville, a few doors above the Nebraska Hotel. 1tf

B. U. ANKENY,

COUNSELLOR AT LAW—Office, Watsonville, Santa Cruz County, Cal. 1tf

P. B. TULLY,

ATTORNEY AT LAW—Office, Gilroy, Santa Clara County, Cal. 1tf

ARTHUR SHEARER.

PEACE!----PEACE!

The following is the concluding portion of Dr. Lindley Spring's pamphlet :

Whatever may be said of these authorities, they certainly dispose of the assertion that those who establish our Government failed to provide against the present crisis, because they could not have foreseen it.

The Union, unbroken, lasted for seventy years and upwards. Under it we prospered greatly. With no other nation has it ever been as with this nation. For the rapidity of its growth, in territorial extent and popular numbers ; in riches and power ; in the diffusion of knowledge ; the development of intelligence ; the cultivation of the sciences and the polite arts ; it has excited the admiration or the jealousy of the civilized world.

Fearless of foreign invasion, confident of our resources, we have thought ourselves secure. Now and then dark clouds have lifted above our horizon, but they seemed to vanish away. Harsh mutterings of domestic discord would be heard, but the sound was too remote and too faint to portend a storm, or our slumbers were too deep to heed the admonition. We indulged bright dreams of perpetual Union, of prosperity without a serious check, and defied consequences. Consequences are avenged ; our vision have been rudely dispelled ; the storm has come upon us ; the temple of our worship totters to its base, and the whole land is under the deepest excitement of anger, apprehension and distress.

To re-establish the Union, and retrieve our fortunes, we have resorted to war—civil war ; the direst calamity which can befall any nation.

Recently, at a public meeting, one who profanely styles himself a *Divine*, invoked this war as *"a war to the knife," and the knife to the hilt."* It was a sentiment fit for the shambles. "And David said unto God. Let us fall now into the hands of the Lord, for His mercies are great ; and let me not fall into the hand of man."

This war has now raged, with great fierceness, for more than eighteen months. The nation has engaged in it with characteristic energy and resolution. There has seemed no limit to the range of violence and destruction. The armed and unarmed, the strong and the weak, the innocent and the guilty, have been alike involved ; and much have we done, and are now doing, which is not war, but vandalism—as if to destroy, and not to restore, was the national purpose. To a very considerable degree we appear to have abandoned the established usage of civilized warfare, and to have adopted the maxims and practices of barbarians, who "considered a state of war as a dissolution of all ties, and a license to every kind of disorder and intemperate fierceness. An enemy was regarded as a criminal and outlaw, who had forfeited his rights...

United States, which declares that "no man shall be held to answer for a capital or other infamous crime, unless on a presentment or indictment of a Grand Jury, nor shall be be deprived of life, liberty or *property*, without due process of law." And that "no attainder of treason shall work forfeiture except during the life of the person attainted."

These things we have done, and more, much more, which will never be disclosed till the graves give up their dead, and men are called to answer the deeds done in the body.

And for what ? To restore the Union ? Well, have we restored it ? Are we any nearer that consummation now than when the war began ? Are we as near ? No ! no ! no ! Such questions mock us ; laugh at our folly, and deride our expectations.

"I could weep for my country when I say that I fear the Union has lost forever its cohesive power. That power lay not so much in its arts or arms ; not in what the Union could produce or defend, but in a kind of mutual recognition of the equality and brotherhood of the great American family, "one and indivisible." All that is gone. For twenty years Northern pulpits and Northern schools have been teaching hatred to the South. That hatred is deep, and, I think, irradicable ; most assuredly, war is not likely to remove the evil. We have had wars which have helped to knit us together ; but a civil war, such as we have on hand now, necessarily uproots everything. I should be glad to believe otherwise, but I cannot" (Extract from a letter of Hon. Thomas H. Seymour, of Conn., to Hon. Nahum Capen of Mass., July 26, 1862.)

How stands the people of the South affected by our remedial process of coercion ? Do they love the Union any better ? Are they any the less united among themselves ? Do they exhibit any signs of yielding, or discouragement, or irresolution ? Is there any abatement of their zeal, energy and courage ? Far from it. They but the more intensely abhor and loath the Union, in whose name immeasurable sufferings and violence have been inflicted on them. Never were they more united, more determined, or more sanguine. They never manifested greater zeal, energy and devotion. Never were they inspired by loftier courage. And besides, they are aided by a spirit which cannot, in the nature of things, animate us ; they fight for their lives, and for their homes, and for all that makes life and home precious.

Are these our hopes of a restoration ? "Do men gather grapes of thorns, and figs of thistles ?"

In the letter of Hon. Robert Dale Owen, to the Hon. Salmon P. Chase, published in a recent number of the Evening Post, occurs the following passage :

"Never since the world began did nine...

a waste of blood and ashes, and resistance has ceased ; the Union has triumphed, and desolation reigns ; the victors have returned laden with spoil ? What then ? Will not the spoil be as the spoil of Achan—an accursed thing ? Will the triumph bring renown, esteem, and a return of peaceful, prosperous, happy days ? Will it restore the Union with its precious gifts ? No ! never ! 'Twere a mischievous delusion to believe it. The desolation we have inflicted, as an avenging spirit, will follow us ; the voice of our brother's blood will cry out against us from the ground ; a guilty conscience will reproach us ; the keen anguish of remorse will smite us ; a hissing, and a reproach, and a by-word shall we become to the nations. When these evils come upon us, then shall we begin to realize the fortune we have blasted ; the ruin we have madly invoked ; the warnings we have contemptuously slighted. Then will

"the sense of lost happiness
And lasting pain torment and overwhelm us ;" reproach and recrimination, wrath and jealousy suspicion and dislike will arise, instead of Peace.

Strange elements these, of Union between Sovereign States, whose changed relation to the whole and to each other cause their conflicting interests to grow daily more impotunate.

The old Union, with its superior benefits, half destroyed and blotted out, where is the cohesive force to bind in one, the jaring fragments ? Shall we find it in an immense public debt ? and which of the States pay it ! Those who allege a failure of the conditions on which it was incurred ? Those who have realized the benefits, or those who have suffered the loss ? Shall we find it in national pride ? That is humble in the dust—or strength and greatness ? They have passed away ; little remains of them, but the violence of the whirlwind, more dangerous to ourselves than to others. In our liberties ? Already they have fled the Capitol. In superior national benefits ! what are they ! name them. In a wronged, deluded, over taxed and distressed people ? The allusion may well excite our hopes. In foreign dangers ? They are remote and speculative. Who will heed them in the turmoil of conflicting passion ! Shall we find it in the desolate South ? Unless human nature has greatly changed, history and experience greatly mistaken, those coveted possession will prove the source of discord, jealously and contention. In any or all of these things do we find full assurance of Hope for our Country ? Alas ! no ! rather the deepest despair.

In contemplating such a future, how dismal is the view—confusion and chaos—society at war with itself—the sword of the smiter turned against his own breast. At such a spectacle, the Genius of Liberty...

Illegal Enlistments.

The fierce emulation and zeal that have marked recruiting efforts in some portions of New England, particularly of Massachusetts, to save certain of the people who owe military duty to the Government, has attracted the attention of other section, and brought down ridicule and opposition. The ridicule, in a good many instances, is richly deserved. In the first year of the war recruiting went forward with wonderful enthusiasm. The contingents came from bones and muscle of the State ; the skilled artisans and the laborers threw down the implements of their industry and seized the weapons of war. When the government call for help, their hearts and hands responded with a cheerful will. They were not for the most part, noisily demonstrative men, and did not spend their time in proclaiming their patriotism or their views of the war. It was enough for them that the nation was in danger and wanted men and they went. Now after three years have passed, and recruits have become scarce, while the exigency of the government is as great as ever, the stay-at-homes still remain at home, but are moving heaven and earth to obtain others to go in their stead.

It is a matter of record that these very people have been foremost in their zeal to induce others to enlist ; foremost in their demands for a vigorous prosecution of the war ; foremost in degrading the war from a contest for the salvation of the country, by the restoration of the Union, to a narrow, radical war of sections and for race ; foremost in upholding the subjugation and emancipation policy ; and now, when the time arrives for them to go, they won't budge an inch. To save themselves, they willingly degrade the State, as they have shown themselves willing to degrade the country, by going into the market and buying flesh and blood, as they would buy beef at the shambles. For this purpose agents are sent to other States and elsewhere, wherever there may be an opportunity to engage in this novel traffic in the bodies of men. But the traffic has attracted attention, and the authorities of other States will no longer permit Massachusetts to enjoy this trade. In Maryland, the District of Columbia and Kentuckey, the agents of Massachusetts have been warned desist from their attempt at illegal enlistments, and Now New York has brought her laws to bear against them. Two agents of this State have been arrested in New York city, indicated by Grand Jury under a law of the State, brought before the Superior Court, and sentenced to fifteen day's imprisonment and $100 fine each. The Judge remarked, in passing sentence, that as these were the first convictions under the law, the penalty would be light. He desired to have it understood, however, that any other cases of illegal...

EXECUTIVE MANSION, WASHINGTON.
July 18, 1864

TO WHOM IT MAY CONCERN: Any proposition which embraces the restoration of peace, the integrity of the whole Union, *and the abandonment of slavery*, and which comes by and with an authority that can control the armies now at war against the United States, will be received and considered by the Executive Government of the United States, and will be met by liberal terms on substantial and collateral points, and the bearer or bearers thereof shall have safe conduct both ways.

ABRAHAM LINCOLN.

ALL FOR THE NEGRO.

We are taxed on our clothing, our meat and bread,
On our carpets and dishes, our tables and beds,
On our tea and our coffee; our fuel and lights,
And we're taxed so severely we can't sleep o' nights.
And it's all for the nigger. Great God! can it be
The home of the brave and the land of the free?

We are stamped on our mortgages, notes, checks and bills,
On our deeds, on our contracts, and on our last will ;
And the Star Spangled Banner in mourning doth wave
O'er the wealth of the nation turned into the grave.
And it's all for the nigger, &c.

We are taxed on our offices, our stores and our shops,
Our stoves and our tin-ware, our brooms and our mops,
Our horses and cattle ; and, if we should die,
We are taxed on the coffins in which we must lie.
And it's all for the nigger, &c.

We are taxed on all goods by kind Providence given;
We are taxed for the Bible that points us to heaven;
And, when we ascend to the heavenly goal,
They would, if they could, *stick a stamp on our soul.*
And it's all for the nigger, &c.

But this is not all; not the money alone
Does the rail-splitter claim for to build up his throne—
If you haven't three hundred, your body must tell,
And if killed in a month, it's all very well
And it's all for the nigger, &c.

Now, boys, will you tell me just what it has cost
To elect old Abe Lincoln and all his black host ?
Just eight hundred thousand—our country's best blood—

On October 8, 1864, the first newspaper was published at San Juan. Only one copy (Vol. I, No. 2) of the paper has been found. The Journal *was obviously published to present the viewpoint of the Confederacy. As such, No.2 may have been the last issue. Publisher B.B. Baker may have lost heart if local support was weak.*

An 1868 map of San Juan shows that a B. B. Barker had owned six acres of land near the cemetery at the west end of Third Street. It was obvious that he had died in the interim as it was listed as "the estate of B. B. Barker."

Local writers probably considered the newspaper a political gesture and the personal opinion of one local secessionist. The advertising supported this; the advertisements were professional cards of men all over the central coast area.

The paper did report on a recent addition of a school in San Juan. In 1860 the Reverend Francis Mora was transferred to Los Angeles where he later became the bishop of the diocese. He was succeeded at San Juan by the Reverend Antonio Ubach, who was considered a "schoolman" by his contemporaries. Within a year Ubach had induced the Sisters of Charity to open an orphanage and day school at the mission. Some have called this the first such school, but records show that San Juan's first school was established in the 1840s for Spanish-speaking boys. Hilario Ortiz was the teacher and there were twelve students. It is not known how long it operated.

The *Journal* carried a news item about the new school: "The Fair held by the Sisters of Charity, for the benefit of the orphans under their care, was a very pleasant affair. The Fair still goes on and we are unable to give further report."

The sisters ran an announcement that they were offering a "Boarding School for Young Ladies." No mention is made of a day school or orphanage.

The school had moved into a "New Building," they announced, and could accept a large number of children. This building was probably the large building behind the church where single Indian women were housed in the mission years. This and another building constructed about this time were used for schools or orphanages until the twentieth century. Earlier the school occupied the cloister or monastery.

Preparations for the Union troops in San Juan were not interrupted by the first newspaper in the area. Arrangements were made to rent the National Hotel for barracks. The post was named Camp Low, for then-governor Frederick F. Low.

When the troops arrived there were three army companies, two infantry and one cavalry, under the command of Major J. C. Cremory. They marched into town and bivouacked on the plaza.

The officers lived at the Plaza Hotel, and some units of enlisted men lived in tents north of the mission rather than in the National Hotel. The guard house also had a liberal attendance every night.

Townspeople became used to the daily morning reveille and dress parade on the plaza. The cavalry often presented mounted drills on the flat north of

---

NOTICE TO THE PUBLIC!

Boarding School for Young Ladies.

THE
SISTERS OF CHARITY,
SAN JUAN, MONTEREY COUNTY,

Having moved into their New Building, they will have ample accommodations for a large number of Children. The rates for Board, Washing, Lodging and Tuition are reduced to the following low figures:

For Board and Tuition, for a year, in Orthography, Reading, Writing, Arithmetic, Grammar, Geography, (with maps and the use of globes,) composition, Natural Philosophy, &c., &c., Spanish Language, and Plain sewing, (payable, half in advance) $150
Washing............................24
Beds and bedding (unless furnished by parents) 12
German Language.........................25
Tapestry, Embroidery, and Ornamental Needlework, each...........................6
Music will also be taught when there are a sufficent number of scholars.

The Sisters of Charity are wholly devoted to Education, and spare no pains to inculcate solid virtue, while they impart useful instruction to those entrusted to their care. The young ladies will be constantly under their supervision, and will be instructed not only in the various branches of polite literature, but in the most useful knowledge of domestic duties and household management.

Parents desirous of entrusting their children to them, would do well to send them previous to the opening of the Institution.

San Juan, Oct. 1804.

From the second edition of the first newspaper to be published in San Juan Bautista.

the mission orchard while most of the townspeople watched from the bluff above.

The troops, both enlisted men and officers, brought outside "strange money" to bars and gambling tables, all of which was welcomed by local businessmen and gamblers.

Crime was not the sole reason for bringing in the troops. Miss Flint wrote of the period saying the townspeople [on] "the turbulent streets of San Juan with their conflicting loyalties, their clandes-

The telegraph came to San Juan. A rare picture in the early 1860s of the newly rebuilt Plaza Hotel, the telegraph pole installed in 1859, the year telegraph service came to the city, and a small portion of the Wells Fargo Express building (far right), which also housed the post office, telegraph office, and the San Juan Drug Store of R. R. Brotherton, who later was listed as an attorney.

tine meetings, and their widely suspect plans were held in day-to-day equilibrium by an encampment of blue-uniformed troops."

Minor friction between a few soldiers and local people was accepted as a necessary burden to endure in exchange for the first real law-and-order force in the area. Lawlessness quickly subsided as scouting parties scoured the area for Mason and Henry or anyone else of questionable character.

There are two stories of a shootout between troopers and Mason and Henry. One was part of a rather long series of events in San Juan that ended

with an unexpected flushing out of the criminals, who fled in an exchange of gunfire. Yet, it seems unlikely that the prime fugitives would have come into town with soldiers on the street.

The other story, as reported by Mylar, is more likely. He wrote, "It was while searching for these three men (secession agitators) who had escaped that a squad of soldiers, away up in the mountains, under the command of Lieutenant Rafferty, came upon the two rascals whose depredations had originally brought troops to San Juan. After a running fight of several miles the two fugitives escaped in the wilderness."

The end of both stories was the same, and Mason and Henry moved on to Fresno County for more wanton killings. They went south and later Henry was killed in San Bernardino County and Mason in the Tejon Pass country.

The troops were removed in April 1865, and peace came once more to San Juan.

San Juan had its share of not-so-good guys—mostly petty thieves and occasionally a murderer. Hangings were not common in San Juan, but there were several. A member of a pioneer family which settled on the Alameda said in 1933 that most of the hangings were from the third willow tree from town, which had a big branch that hung out over the Alameda.

Dates, names and details were seldom handed down. An unnamed sheepherder was killed for money he was known to carry. Citizens, unnamed of course, "made a good citizen" out of an unnamed murderer by hanging him. End of the story.

How many times this happened we don't know and never will. For several reasons this vigilante action is not surprising. San Juan was at the crossroads of California, and most early bandits passed through, some undoubtedly stopping for spending money. There were no police, deputy sheriff or constable in all of eastern Monterey County for at least fifty years. Take the killer to Salinas for trial? This meant a two-day trip for the captors with the accused, and the same for witnesses at the trial.

Speedy justice may have its merits, but it also has its dangers. An unnamed patron in Riggin's Saloon, while roaring drunk, burst out of the saloon with a pistol in hand, announcing his intentions of shooting somebody. The street was deserted so he stumbled up to Third Street. As he turned the corner he met Manuel Butron, who often had epileptic seizures. He shot Butron squarely in the chest and Butron collapsed on the sidewalk.

People were able to disarm the drunk and take him into custody. Butron was bleeding profusely, so the crowd agreed that the drunk should be hanged from a willow tree on the Alameda. He requested a priest, and one was brought from the mission. After they talked, the crowd proceeded to the execution which had been so speedily decided upon.

When the men returned to the saloon they discovered Butron had not died. He not only lived, but

ATTENTION!

ARMY ORDERS.

SanJuan is now in the State of Martial Law.

Headquarters, Department of the Pacific
Benicia, January 23, 1865

SPECIAL ORDER NUMBER 17

Due to the increasing activities of the despicable Southern Loyalists, the Sixth California Infantry Volunteers, Company G, has been ordered to march from Benicia to Camp Low San Juan, California to quell any disturbances that may arise.

Date of arrival, 2 February 1865

By command of 1ST LT William J. Newley
Sixth California Infantry Volunteers
Company G·

Major Michael O'Brien, District Commander

The disturbances never materialized and not a shot was fired, except maybe at some suspected criminals.

he never again had a seizure. We are assured by Mylar that "the hanging . . . rested heavily on the conscience of some of the men who so promptly executed summary justice on the poor devil," still unnamed.

Fire was a serious threat in all early California towns, but San Juan was quite fortunate in that regard, probably because so many buildings were constructed of adobe, brick or fire resistant redwood. The town's luck ran out at about 4:00 A.M. on November 1, 1867. A fire was discovered in Dan Harris' New Idria Store at the southwest corner of Third and Mariposa streets. The store was destroyed at a loss to Harris of $35,000. The fire continued west on Third Street, wiping out several smaller buildings. Only Harris had insurance, which reimbursed him just $12,000.

One of the most serious misfortunes to hit San Juan in the late 1860s was an epidemic such as is hardly imaginable now. In 1868 it was brought upon the town by one man: a visitor from Los Angeles who was stopping at the National Hotel.

The man became sick and a doctor's diagnosis was measles. Thoughtful citizens visited him to offer food and comfort. One of them was James Collins, a badly pock-marked man. He got one look and said, "If that man hasn't smallpox then I never had it."

Unfortunately, a big dance was held in town, attended by many townspeople. Forty dancers reportedly came down with smallpox, and it spread like wildfire.

Some families took off to the mountains and camped out. Mylar said the town was quarantined, with all roads into town barred. On one night thirteen people died, and during the epidemic "upwards of 130 died of the disease." This was probably about 25 percent of the population.

Provisions ran low in town until two men volunteered to go to Monterey for help. They changed to clean clothes before entering Monterey, but when the townspeople learned who they were they ran from them. A "kind" doctor vouched for the safety of talking to the men. When the people learned of their needs they responded very generously with supplies and money.

The *Monterey Gazette* of November 19, 1868, reported: "We learn that Mr. W. R. Parker has collected and forwarded to San Juan the sum of $120.00 for the relief of the sufferers of that town. Of this amount Castroville contributed $65.00 and Salinas $55.00."

Two months later the *Gazette* of January 21, 1869, reported that there was no more smallpox in San Juan.

Dr. C. A. Canfield also reported that he had vaccinated 650 persons during the past few months in Monterey.

No mention was made about what the seven stage lines that came through San Juan did during the epidemic. There may have been a road through Monterey, but it would have been longer and the stages would not have wanted to go through Watsonville, which also was hit hard by the smallpox. That route would have been made even more difficult as a bridge on the road between Watsonville and Santa Cruz had been wrecked by frightened Santa Cruz men who panicked and tore it out so no one could bring the pox to their city.

As bad as the epidemic was, there was a story of good fortune that came out of it. The dead were taken to the cemetery at night, and lights of lanterns could be seen darting around the cemetery as people buried the dead. One night the wagon was going along the Alameda on its way from the pesthouse to the cemetery. The creek often created a marshy area along the Alameda, and rocks had to be put in to make the road passable. The wagon this night jolted over a big rock and caused a coffin to slide off the wagon. The "dead" man came to in the water and clambered out of the coffin. He lived for many years, though badly pock-marked.

The story is vouched for by the Wilcox family, who lived on the Alameda for many years.

Almost all other histories make no mention of the epidemic, but one matched brevity with inaccuracy in one sentence: "In 1868 this village was wiped out entirely by smallpox."

San Juan had a little luck in October 1868. There was a rather severe earthquake which was centered about fifty miles to the north, and while it was a good shake, it caused little damage to San Juan.

As the state grew so also did San Juan. By 1868 there were enough people in the eastern side of Monterey County to arouse interest in the area to have a county of its own. It was costly to cross the mountains any time a person had business in the county offices, and the lack of law enforcement was growing critical.

San Juan started to correct this situation on two fronts in 1868. On the local level plans were initiated to incorporate the town, and San Juan joined other towns in the area in plans to form a new county: San Benito.

By October 9, 1869, the town was incorporated as "The Inhabitants of the Town of San Juan." The first elected trustees were David Harris, Peter Breen, J. F. Black, George Pullen, and Juan B. Carriega. Harris was elected president and Breen secretary.

On November 3, 1869, they authorized some salaries. A marshal, who was also the exofficio pound master, was to receive fifty dollars a month; the assessor forty dollars plus one-fourth of 1 percent of the taxes; and the treasurer 4 percent of the taxes.

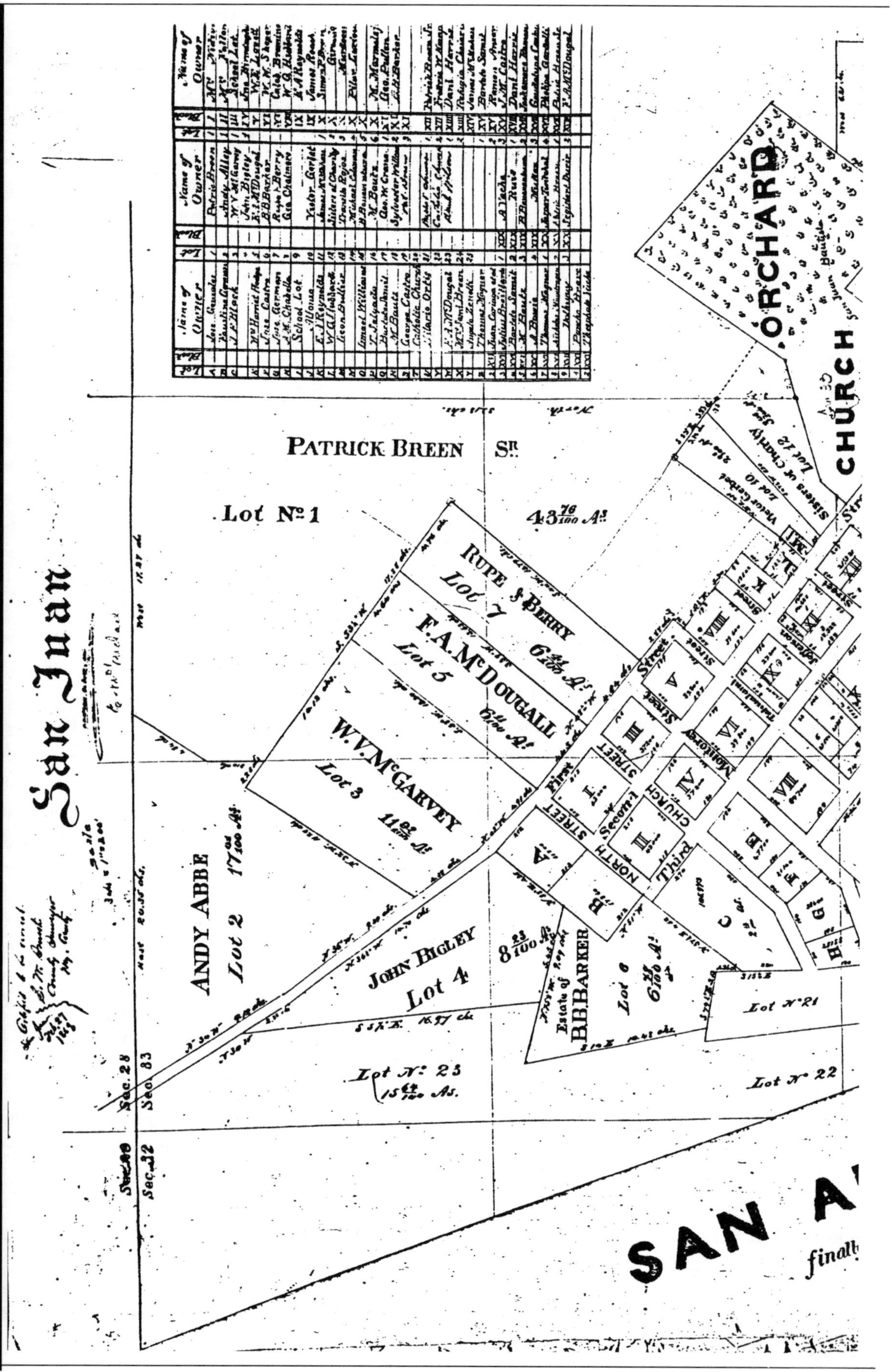

SAN JUAN BAUTISTA — 1869

San Juan

PATRICK BREEN ST.

Lot No 1   43 76/100 A.

RUPE & PERRY   Lot 7

F. A. M^c DOUGALL   Lot 5

W. V. M^c GARVEY   Lot 3   11 62/100 A.

ANDY ABBE   Lot 2   17 00/100 A.

JOHN BIGLEY   Lot 4   8 23/100 A.

Estate of B. B. BARKER   Lot 6   6 25/100 A.

Lot No 23   15 70/100 As.

Lot No 21

Lot No 22

ORCHARD

CHURCH

SAN A

finally

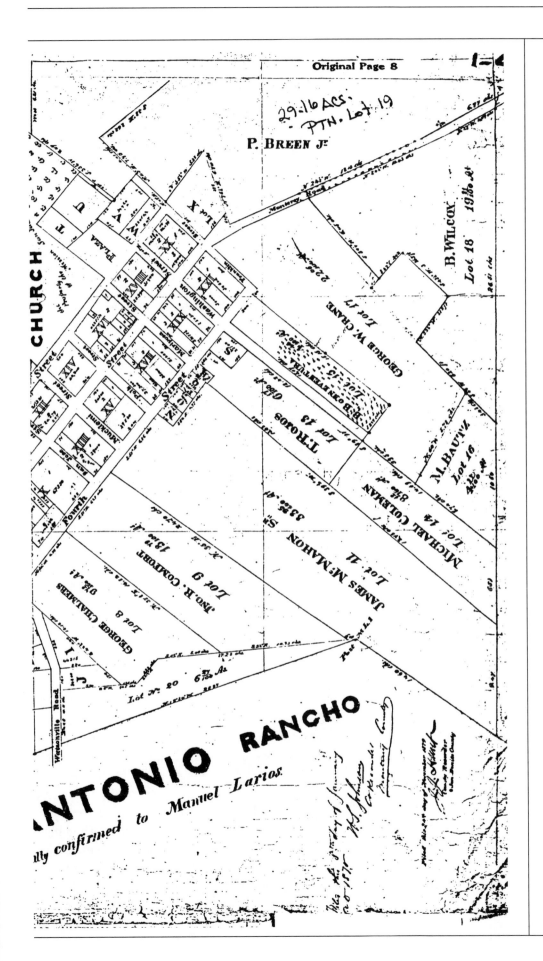

This certified map of the San Juan district dated February 27, 1868, was filed with the Monterey County recorder November 24, 1869, apparently as part of the incorporation the previous month of "the inhabitants of the Town of San Juan." At the top was written, "Certified to be correct. S. W. Smith, County Surveyor, Monterey County, Feb. 27, 1868." At the bottom, "Filed the 24th day of November, 1869, W. S. Johnson, County Recorder, Monterey County." The unusual notation "finally confirmed" reflects the community's interest in the long delayed decision on this and other land grants by José Castro. The Larios family donated the land for the San Juan cemetery.

A speed limit also was established. No rider should "ride here in a furious speed" or he might be fined from five dollars to one hundred dollars.

The minutes were limited to business transacted, not to discussions or plans for the future. They were brief and to the point; for example, in May 1879 the trustees voted sixty-four dollars for "burial of a Chinaman" (no name). Many meetings had practically no minutes.

The new city's board of trustees continued to function, enacting laws to clean up the language as well as the streets of the town. People might be fined five to ten dollars for a variety of misdemeanors such as:

a) . . . fighting, assaulting, beating or bruising a person or inhumanely abusing any horse, mule or ox.

b) Indecent conduct in words, or unnecessarily firing any gun or pistol.

c) Storing wagons, carts or wood on city streets.

d) . . . any drunkards unable to walk or . . . so drunk as to lie down on any sidewalk, street, hotel, saloon, outhouse, orchard either in public or private.

There were other rather routine laws, all of which were up to the town marshal to enforce. He also was expected to see that the town was kept clean.

For the first two years no one held the job very long, due to the "unhealthiness" of it. A local newspaper reported September 7, 1870: "The town marshal was somewhat surprised on Saturday evening last, by hearing a bullet whistle in close proximity to his head. The man who fired it missed his mark. We understand this is the fourth time he has been taken for a target."

A town jail was built in June 1870, street signs were put up in September, and a firehouse was built the next year. All this was accomplished with city funds, as was the planting of trees along the main streets.

No mention was made of the plans for a new county, but the trustees were undoubtedly supportive and fully confident that San Juan was going to be the county seat. Events during this period prevented the latter from happening.

By 1868, Colonel William Wells Hollister and the owners of Flint-Bixby & Company had grown to be the most powerful group in the area.

Benjamin Flint, Dr. Thomas Flint and Llewellyn Bixby, a cousin of the Flints, were all from Maine. They were early and successful entrants in the Gold Rush of 1849. They took their wealth with them and returned to Maine, but, impressed with the opportunities in California, they decided to return.

In March 1853 they formed a partnership and purchased sheep to bring to California. They arrived with 2,400 sheep in San Jose in March 1854 before making San Juan their permanent home. They made their first purchase of land here in 1855.

On April 15, 1839, General Jose Castro was granted a huge 34,615-acre grant known as the San Justo Grant. As might be expected, General Castro's grant included the choicest land in the county. The grant was nearly square and extended across the valley with the San Benito River running down the middle. It extended from about three miles east of San Juan to about five miles beyond the future site of Hollister.

Castro was a soldier, not a farmer, so, as with his other grants, he sold the land before processing it to receive a patent. In this case he sold the San Justo to Don Francisco P. Pacheco for a reported $1,400.

On October 2, 1855, Flint-Bixby & Company and Colonel Hollister bought the land from Don Pacheco. The price quoted by author Dorothy Flint was $25,000. Some have quoted $14,000, which is probably confused with the Castro sale. Others say $17,000 and like to add that it was less than fifty cents an acre. At $25,000 the cost would have been seventy-one cents an acre; still a pretty good bargain for the partners.

During the following years Flint-Bixby & Company and San Justo prospered and were a constructive element in San Juan's development. However, a division of San Justo which was started in 1861 and completed in 1868 resulted in a sale that led to a most serious depression for the town of San Juan.

Flint-Bixby & Company and Colonel Hollister signed an agreement November 30, 1861, that Hollister would receive about 20,773 acres of the eastern portion of San Justo, and the other partners would retain the smaller western lands. Necessary surveys and legal documents were not completed and signed until April 14, 1866.

Within two years Hollister negotiated the sale of his acreage to the newly-formed San Justo Homestead Association for $370,000. The association proceeded to divide the land into fifty-one lots. Fifty would be for farms and pastures, and the fifty-first for a townsite. The town was named Hollister and was completely laid out by November of 1868.

The creation of another town did not in itself threaten San Juan, but two outgrowths of the new city quickly posed serious problems for San Juan.

First, the railroad from San Francisco reached Gilroy in 1869 and everyone knew of the intention to continue south. Flint-Bixby & Company had been in touch with the railroad as early as 1863, when they wrote to friends in Maine that "next Monday we have a meeting to organize a company to build a railroad from San Jose this way . . . "

It is doubtful that "this way" meant "to San Juan" then, and it certainly did not five years later. The railroad wanted a $60,000 subsidy, including a right of way, to build its line to San Juan. The San Justo partners, who must have known how valuable the train would be, used their influence to persuade sheep and cattle men to oppose the subsidy. The businessmen could not do it alone. Hollister won the railroad, as we now know, but in 1869 and 1870 the people of San Juan thought that surely the railroad would be routed through San Juan, or at worst on a route three or four miles west of town.

The *Monterey Gazette* of June 8, 1869, included a short article listing the businesses then in San Juan. It did not say it was a report of the zenith of business in the town, but from a vantage point of more than a hundred and twenty years, we know San Juan was nearing its top population at that point.

The newspaper reported: "Nine stores with a general assortment of merchandise, eight saloons and billiard rooms, two hotels, two barbers, two express offices, one telegraph office, one physician, two lawyers, two public halls and two occupied by Masons and Odd Fellows." A competitive spirit apparently prompted the writer to omit from the list a newspaper or two which were possibly publishing in San Juan at that time.

Rome Ranch of Luigi Raggio near San Juan from an engraving in the 1881 Elliott & Moore History of San Benito County. It may be called typical of the thirty or more engravings in the book.

The railroad reached Gilroy in 1869, and as that town expanded, San Juan lost freight and stagecoach traffic to the New Idria mines, the new and growing town of Hollister, and the farms in the eastern and southern part of the county.

However, San Juan was well established, and in 1870 many people still believed the town would benefit from the extension of the railroad to the south of Gilroy. They were also certain the town was destined for even greater growth as the seat of the new county when it was formed. After all, it was the only incorporated town in the area.

In 1870 one notable addition was made to the businesses of San Juan. Hereafter the town would, for many years, have its own good beer as well as its own good wine.

Jake Beuttler, a brewer, came to town and established a brewery on the north side of Third Street at its junction with the Alameda.

Working with his stepson, Fred Beck, he produced a fine quality beer which was popular throughout the area. Before long he was delivering a regular route through Hollister, Bell Station, San Luis (where the B.F. Sisk-San Luis Dam is now), Los Banos, Dos Palos, and Firebaugh's Ferry.

In 1875, a fire did serious damage to the brewery and he moved operations to the old grist mill on

San Justo Rancho south of town as it was in 1881. The buildings, left to right, are: horse barn, original house where Col. Hollister and his sister lived earlier, sheep barn, and the residence of the three families of Flint, Bixby & Company. The families moved from the small house in February 1863. Public access to the area is closed. This drawing was prepared for the History of San Benito County, California with Illustrations, 1881*, Elliott & Moore, publishers.*

Fourth Street which he purchased from merchant Daniel Harris.

Beuttler moved his family across Third Street to the Anzar Adobe, one of the town's oldest buildings, which later passed to his stepson Fred Beck. It was used as a residence with only occasional commercial use during most of the years until 1933 when San Juan's first antique store was opened there.

The antique store at 103 Third Street is still in the hands of a Beck. When Charles A. Beck returned from service in the Army, he acquired the property from the estate of Fred Beck. He has continued to operate one of the best stores in one of the oldest buildings in town.

The brewery building is still across the street but is a private residence with no resemblance to a brewery.

Jake Beuttler and his wife had three children: George, Albert, and Annie. Annie married a man who arrived about a year after Jake and who was the town's outstanding personality for fifty-seven years. His name was Mark Regan.

Regan was born in 1847 in Missouri. He ran away from home when he was fourteen and joined the Confederate Army.

Regan set up his own stage line in San Juan for local needs. His initial route was to Hollister and Sargent Station, the Southern Pacific's transfer point for passengers to San Juan. He varied the route as needed but always on a local basis. When the time came, he "graduated" to autos and small buses.

It was not Regan's service or skill as a driver that made him "known far and wide." People vied for a chance to ride next to him so they could have the full benefit of his jokes, storytelling and anec- dotes about local history. He was always ready to lend a helping hand and appears to have been liked and respected by all.

It is unfortunate that Regan did not keep a diary as he was an early member of the Texas Lodge of Ma- sons and well-informed about all San Juan activities. His di- ary would be as good as com- plete files of a couple of news- papers.

A search for contempo- rary newspapers resulted in the discovery of fourteen newspapers of the 1870-1880 era in San Juan. They have given us some insights into local life but none on the great exodus of businesses and people from San Juan in 1871. Microfilm copies of the newspapers were obtained from the Bancroft Library, Univer- sity of California at Berkeley, in June 1993.

Newspapers in that era had a fairly uniform for- mat without pictures, much art or national wire ser- vice. The front page carried limited advertising, national and international news, and possibly liter- ary work, including poems. The second page car- ried editorials, the masthead, and news, usually re- gional or local. Pages three and four carried most of the advertisements, with local news under various headings, more often on page four. The out-of-town news was old and pretty dull, at least by present-

day standards. There was not much politics dis- cussed except in the pro-secessionist *Monterey County Journal*, which strongly opposed the reelec- tion of President Lincoln.

San Juan was generally credited with being the smallest town in the west to ever have four local

For over thirty years Mark Regan was a dependable stagecoach operator and driver. The routes varied, but they never expanded beyond San Juan, Gilroy, Hollister, and train transfer points. Regan boosted San Juan at every opportunity and had a wealth of stories about local incidents, personalities and history with which he loved to regale his passengers.

Photo: SJB Historical Society Public Archives

newspapers at one time. Those four were undoubt- edly the *San Juan Central Californian*, *San Juan Echo*, *San Juan Valley Echo*, and the *San Juan Star*. They all were published in 1871, but it is quite pos- sible they were not all publishing in any one week or month.

Some insight into the fate of at least one of these papers was given in a latter-day newspaper, the *Voice of San Juan Bautista*, on April 16, 1971. The "Bits of Old News" column of the *Voice* on that date included a reprint of an interview with Mayor Frank B. Abbe with a dateline of Hollister, May 9 (no year was given, but it would have appeared in the late 1920s or early 1930s). He was credited with coming "to the front with a solution of the mystery surrounding the disappearance of the *San Juan Central Californian* . . . [which] disappeared in the fall of 1871 . . . According to the San Juan mayor, the owners, Byerley and Clevenger, just packed up their scanty equipment and moved overnight to Salinas, where they started a paper that was the forerunner of the *Salinas Index.*"

The mayor gave the 1870 population of San Juan as 2,638 and of Hollister at about four hundred. By 1872 the populations had reversed, to about four hundred in San Juan and over two thousand in Hollister. In the interview Mayor Abbe also was recognized as an "amateur newspaper publisher" for his role in publishing the 1880 *Argonaut.*

Of the other three newspapers, we have proof of the publication of the *San Juan Echo* only, of which there are thirteen weekly copies extant from November 16, 1870, to March 14, 1871. Two issues in January and two later issues are missing from the series.

The *Echo* was founded September 7, 1870, by Hiram C. Hazen, a printer on Fourth Street who moved to Third Street in December. The publication office was on Second Street next to the National Hotel.

Hazen edited the first ten editions, but on November 16, 1870, A. D. Jones became a partner and editor. Jones was the former publisher and editor of the *Kern County Courier.* He added the Latin watchwords *Festina Lente* (hasten slowly) under the paper's name.

The extension of the railroad south from Gilroy received slight attention in the *Echo.* In the November 16, 1870, edition a column headed "Our Hollister Letter" started with, "Railroad matters are still quiet." Period!

On December 3 the paper ran the following article:

ROUTE OF SOUTHERN PACIFIC RAILROAD

The Southern Pacific Railroad Company is about to commence work on a section of twenty miles of railroad extending south from Gilroy. We have not learned that the final location of the sections of road beyond the points mentioned have yet been made. But the *Sacramento Record*, which is in a special sense, we believe, the organ of the Central Pacific Company, suggests the following route:

The third, and the one that likely has been selected, is that from Gilroy through a pass in the mountains to the Salinas Valley [and south to San Diego and east to Mojave].

This route would have been a halfway victory for San Juan, but it was not to be. The Southern Pacific had a dream of a transcontinental line through Hollister, south to Fresno County and then over the Sierra Nevada mountains in competition to the Central Pacific.

Two months later, on February 4, 1871, an extension of time by the railroad was reported, and an unidentified letter writer said, "Gilroy will continue to be the terminal for three years . . . and Hollister will grow with farm produce."

In the next-to-final edition Editor Jones announced that he had become the publisher. He expressed his intentions to continue publication of the newspaper. In the last two editions, March 4 and March 14, Jones explained that recent delays resulted from the failure of a printer to arrive from San Jose as promised. The lack of experienced help may be the reason for some of these pages being noted as "original defective" on the microfilm.

Thomas McMahon has been mentioned as one of the first businessmen to close his store and move to Hollister. It may be significant that he had the largest advertisement in the newspapers, offering "a Large and Well Selected Stock . . . at the Lowest Prices! And on the Most Reasonable Terms." Eight major assortments of "a Large and Selected Stock . . . Usually Found in a Well Assorted Country Store" are attractively presented by the printer in one column of the type nearly a foot long. This was many years before pictures could be printed. Engravings for art were expensive, and merchants seldom used them or quoted prices.

I. F. Roth advertised his store, The Pearl of San Juan, in much the same format, but less than half as large. He said he was offering all his merchandise "At Ruinously Low Prices."

Julius Brietbarth offered boots and shoes in a similar ad, offering all at the "Very Lowest Prices."

M. Filousheau's General Merchandise Store also advertised goods "At Uncommonly Low Prices." Forsaking the usual policy, he priced Theophilus Vache's wine "at 50 cents per gallon."

Do these advertisements mark the beginning of the exodus from San Juan? It may be just a little early, but there are no more newspapers to tell us.

The editor found great hope in a discovery announced January 28, 1871:

COAL DISCOVERY

Dr. Mathews, of this place, has given us information of an important discovery—one which if it proves as rich as we have reason to hope and believe it will, is destined to add immensely to the wealth of this county.

The discovery is nothing less than a mine of coal, about thirty miles from San Juan in a Southeasterly direction. The lead has been traced about six miles, and from all appearances the supply is almost inexhaustible.

It has been tried in the blacksmith shop of Mr. Ouderkirk and is pronounced a superior article.

This discovery may justly be regarded as one of the first of importance to this county. . . . The question of how fuel is to be obtained is one of momentous interest, and as the forests are being stripped of their supply of fuel the question becomes more and more important. *A good coal mine is of vastly more importance than a gold mine.*

It is nice to know that over a hundred years ago they were concerned about forests.

During the time encompassed by these newspapers the fall session at the local schools ended and the spring session commenced. This gives us an insight into education in the 1870s which otherwise would not have been available.

In addition to the public schools there was one parochial and one private school. No further information on the last two was published.

The 1870 fall term ended with a public series of examinations on Wednesday, November 30, and continued for three days. The *Echo* reported, "The spelling and defining of a thousand words will commence at 10 A.M. and 2 P.M. each day . . . other branches from 9-10 A.M. and from 1 to 2 P.M."

The *Echo* reported the school exhibition on Friday evening in Plaza Hall, which the public was urged to attend. The thirty-one exhibits were:

1. Laconics.
2. Declamation.
3. Mistletoe bough.
4. Darius Green and his Flying Machine.
5. Charade.
6. Tableau, About Ben Adhem and the Angel.
7. Declamation, Napoleon at rest.
8. The Twelve Months.
9. Young Orator.
10. The Little Speaker.
11. The Flag of Our Union.
12. Tableau, Tom Thumb and his Wife.
13. Who Stole the Nest?
14. Early Rising.
15. Red, White and Blue.
16. Joan of Arc at the Stake.
17. Mrs. Jarley's Wax Works.
18. Night and Morning.
19. Hohen Linden.
20. Widow's Mistake.
21. The Cold Water Man.
22. Who Bit My Apple?
23. The Removal.
24. Woman's Rights.
25. Little Red Riding Hood.
26. The Satisfactory Answer.
27. John Jones' Fortune.
28. Life Scene.
29. Cinderella.
30. Statuary: Hope, Faith and Charity.
31. Tableau, the Handwriting on the Wall.

The spelling and defining of a thousand words was quite a contest, with a new *Webster's Unabridged Dictionary* as first prize. Other prizes were supplied by public donations.

Principal S. M. Shearer placed great emphasis on spelling and the thousand-word contests. A committee of twelve was appointed to assist in the contest, but when judging began many were missing and others had to be found to help.

The principal assumed the responsibility of selecting the thousand words and reading them to the contestants, who were apparently all the students. No mention was made as to grades or sections, but the newspaper did say that all tests were numbered to "render it impossible that any partiality could be shown" by the judges.

The judges had a herculean task with a thousand basic words and an estimated twenty-five hundred words in the definitions. After a time the com-

THE SAN JUAN ECHO.

"Festina Lente."

VOLUME I.   SAN JUAN, MONTEREY COUNTY, CALIFORNIA, THURSDAY, SEPTEMBER 22, 1870.   NUMBER 2.

The San Juan Echo

IS PUBLISHED AT

San Juan, Monterey Co., Cal.,

EVERY THURSDAY, BY

Hiram C. Hazen

TERMS:

$1.00 a year, in advance.
2.25 for six months.

RATES OF ADVERTISING.

One Square (ten lines or less) Two Dollars for the first insertion, and One Dollar for each subsequent insertion.

A liberal discount made to regular and yearly advertisers.

Special Notices.

To ADVERTISERS:—Special Notices inserted at 20 cents a line first insertion, and 10 cents each subsequent one. Open to advertisers only.

Book and Job Printing

Of every description executed with neatness and despatch at reasonable prices.

TEXAS LODGE, No. 46, F. & A. M. Stated Communications second Saturday evening of each month.

At Masonic Hall, San Juan.

Sojourning Brothers in good standing cordially invited to attend.

CHARLES F. MITCHELL, W. M.
R. M. BROTHERTON, Secretary.

NATIONAL HOTEL.

SAN JUAN, - - - Monterey County.

GEORGE PULLEN,

Proprietor,

THIS FIRST CLASS HOUSE,

So long and favorably known to the traveling public is still open for the accommodation of Guests.

A well-supplied Table, clean, comfortable Beds and moderate prices are the attractions offered: and Patrons of the House can rest assured of receiving every attention. Stages call at this House daily from all parts of the State and County.

San Juan Drug Store,

SECOND STREET, ...SAN JUAN.

Rounds & Ainsworth

Announce to their Friends and the Public that they are opening at the above place

A LARGE STOCK OF

DRUGS, PATENT MEDICINES, OILS, PERFUMERY, TOILET and FANCY ARTICLES, SCHOOL BOOKS, STATIONERY, &c. &c.

Physician's Prescriptions carefully compounded. tf-1

[BY HARRY.]

This tiny old woman in faded black gown,
With her fuzzy gray ness so many and quaint,
So trim and complete from her feet to her crown—
You'd scarcely believe it, but see in my saint.

The clear brown eye grown heavy with care,
The little brown hands the worse for wear,
The thinning streaks of her silvery hair
Are still to my heart unspeakably fair.

Many a year have we journeyed together,
I often despondent, quite heart-sick and faint,
She bravely defying the stormiest weather.—
Herself sweetest sunshine—my glorious saint!

Never a care have I borne alone,
Never in solitude made my moan;
Nearer and nearer the tie has grown,
Flesh of my flesh is she, bone of my bone.

The beauty that dwells in her wrinkled old face,
This poor silly pen of mine never can paint;
'Tis a halo from heaven—a natural grace
For the soul that looks out from the eyes of my saint.

Early and late, by night and by day,
Whether I watch or whether I pray,
That soul still lightens my toilsome way,
Its truth my evangel, its love my stay.

[Written for the San Juan Echo.]

"AFTER MANY DAYS."

BY WESLEY.

"Oh, Memory, give me back those long departed
To shore remote and silent shores unknown,

---

while living! Not till she has been called to her spiritual home, forever from our sight, do we know how to prize the gem we once possessed.

When the world's chilling breath passes over me, and withers the flowers in our youthful hearts, when we seek sympathy and find it not, then do we yearn for her kind sympathizing heart, and weep, when we think that her gentle voice can never more fill our hearts with its sweet music.

Her good night kiss, always sending you to bed happy, whatever came trooping your childish mind. The memory if this in the stormy years of after life will be as the Bethlehem Star to the bewildered shepherd, and swelling up in your heart will rise the thought, my mother loved me. Lips parcbel with fever will become dewy at this the thrill of youthful memories.

Then comes memories of your school days, when your educational advancement was so rapid as to call down the highest encomiums from your tutor, you smile, when you reflect that mother was the incentive.

You remember that you were a timid, retiring child, and at school you were secluded and apart from your vivacious companions, and would retire to the "old oak," sacred to you from its memories, and whilst your companions would make the air ring with their welkin, your mind would revel in wild joyous dreams of the future.

---

earth's another love perhaps may come to you, but it will lack some of the freshness of this sweet delight, some clearness of perfect happiness will be wanting.

The dream was so bright that you had lived in it only. Both past and happy golden dreams of future were over-shadowed, you had never thought of gaining her, except vaguely in the far off future, but now, when you knew you must decide the question, you paced up and down the floor of your room, and with white lips murmured, "I cannot be."

You were extremely sensitive, you never could endure the remarks incident upon so apparent an attachment, by the cold unfeeling world. You were afraid of the world's opinion. These thoughts went wandering up and down through your mind, and although you knew in your heart that these obstacles might be overcome, you thought them over and over, trying to shut out the true reason, but it would force itself upon you.

You slowly arose and mechanically following the beaten path that led to your bower, stood in her presence. She took your hand in her own, looked deep within your eyes, into your soul, and reading there the inevitable decree of fate, said, without reproach, without bitterness, but with such a depth of sorrow in her tender tones:

"Beloved—but not mine."

And then while you stood silent, so silent that it seemed as if the beating of your heart must be audible to her, she

---

she desired a parcel ying upon the table by her bedside to be opened.

You opened it. Unfastening the ribbon that bound it, disclosed a withered rose bud. She grasped it with a smile, as though she had found a long lost treasure and without a word, or look of recognition to you, died.

Died! In her early womanhood, when you loved her as your own soul—that was the bitterest drop in the cup, but you bore it, and said, "Thy will, oh God!" and buried her with holy sorrow, and returning home gave yourself up to tho most poignant grief.

You are aroused from that terrible dream, and under its appalling influences you sit down at your desk and write:

Fathers have mercy,—have mercy upon the future lives of your innocent children. Do not give that moral poison to them in their infancy, sweetened and made palatable to their infant tastes, under the delusion that it will quiet them or soothe their pain. Do not mix its vile flavor in your sauces, your jellies and your creams, to create a taste, which, unless inherited, is seldom, if ever, natural. If you have acquired an unconquerable thirst for it, do not indulge it before them. Warn them faithfully against its resistless, ruthless power, and "they that sow the wind, shall reap the whirlwind," and the poisoned bread which you now "cast upon your heart must be audible to her, she

---

The first page of Vol. 1, No. 2 of The San Juan Echo of September 22, 1870, was reprinted in the San Juan Bautista Echo nearly one hundred years later. This rare page is the only one found of the ten issues edited by publisher Hiram Hazen. It tends to support the sharp criticism of A. D. Jones, later editor and publisher. The typography is fine, but the subject matter is dull, to say the least. Of the six columns, two are advertising (a common practice), one is poetry and the other two tell a tragic love tale of no news value and questionable literary value.

mittee decided to give no further attention to entries with more than twenty errors.

The *Echo* gave details of the results of the best four entries. Out of about thirty-five hundred words, "Miss Huldah Reynolds had six errors consisting of one misspelled basic word, one word in the definitions, one definition not being used, and three words improperly defined.

"Miss Emma Rue had eleven errors of which nine were in definitions, the 'e' in muscle had been erased after it was correctly written, and the definition given for 'behoove' was correct only for 'behoof.'

"Miss Sarah Shepherd misspelled four basic words, one in a definition, and four definitions were improper.

"Master John Mathews misspelled one basic word, one in a definition, nine definitions were improper, and one was no longer in use, for a total of twelve."

The judges were obliged to come back on Monday because of the details involved in such a contest. Also, there were the Friday night exhibits and the dancing afterward at the Plaza Room.

Editor Jones, who had just arrived in town for his new position, was a member of the judging committee and said in conclusion that the contest " . . . in its results shows a degree of proficiency which reflects the greatest credit upon all."

Spelling obviously enjoyed continued importance. On March 4, 1871, the *Echo* carried a list of members of two teams of twenty-two members each. They had competed on the preceding Friday, and Emma Rue and Annie O'Flynn "were found to be most proficient."

This was not only the end of the school year; it was also the holiday season and the end of 1870, an important and later to be known as an unfortunate year for San Juan.

The November and December issues of the *San Juan Echo* had not a single advertisement that mentioned, or even hinted at Christmas shopping. It was not until December 24 that there was mention of it in the news columns. It is true that Editor Jones had been on the job just over a month, but that seems a weak excuse.

On Saturday, the day before Christmas, the *Echo* did have an article about the Christmas festival that had been held the previous evening.

Plaza Hall was crowded "to its utmost capacity and there were three servings of dinner." The menu is not mentioned, but a small news item elsewhere in the paper said that traditional competitive turkey shoots were being held as they went to press.

"Two large trees were loaded with presents for the children—some of them very costly, and it was found that they had no room for the great number that had been sent. It required four or five persons to distribute them."

The concluding paragraph read, "Compare this festival with the bull fights of but a few years ago, and who shall say that San Juan has not taken a big step in the right direction." Since Christmas fell on Sunday, businesses were observing the holiday on Saturday.

Another holiday message was presented in a small news item about the New Year's observance:

"THE BALL. Next Friday the San Juan Brass Band is to give a ball at Plaza Hall. The management of the ball has been entrusted to good hands, and we have no doubt but that it will be a success."

The *Echo* of December 31 and January 7 were not included in the microfilm collection. What little news that appeared in the early months of 1871 has been reviewed in a topical manner. In the last issue we have, dated March 14, 1871, Mr. Jones, now editor and publisher, devotes an entire column to reporting his new status and an "Explanatory" on his five months with the paper.

He was prevailed upon in early November by Mr. Hazen "to come to San Juan and take an interest in the paper." They immediately bought new type for the paper and other printing materials. It soon

became evident that "Hazen's idea of business was so at variance with" his that they could not work together.

A printer was needed so Hazen remained working on wages which, Jones said, "of course vitiated the partnership previously entered into . . . " (of course?) In fourteen weeks this proved a losing proposition for Jones, and when he told Hazen this, Hazen said he would publish the paper himself.

There were apparently two other people involved in the venture as Jones said, "The owners of the material entered a loud protest—both being convinced . . . that Hazen was totally unfitted for the management of a newspaper." Jones claimed that "under Hazen's management the paper was simply a disgrace to journalism . . ." Jones later revealed that he did not have, nor had he even seen, any of the ten editions that Hazen edited and published.

There was more, but this makes it fairly obvious that Jones had not observed the Latin admonition on his front page, *festina lente* ("hasten slowly").

In the March 14, 1871 issue of the *Echo* a reference to the *Central Californian* reveals that Byerley and Clevenger had not yet left for Salinas.

This leaves several questions unanswered. How long was the *San Juan Echo* published? Did one of these men just change the name, for legal reasons, to *San Juan Valley Echo*, which began publication in the next nine months? What was the role of Thomas Hughes and his *San Juan Star*?

Of course, there is then the question about all three newspapers: How long did they continue to publish after the great exodus began?

THE EXODUS
AND AFTER

n Wednesday, August 2, 1871, a quorum of the town trustees was not present for their regular meeting so those in attendance set the meeting over to August 3. On the third, action was set over to the regular meeting in September. This was unheard of!

On September 6, trustees again did not have a quorum and set the meeting over to the seventh, and then to the eighth, and to the ninth, when, with a quorum finally present, the trustees paid two small bills.

The town must have been in a turmoil, and the trustees undoubtedly were reflecting the general discouragement of the rest of the citizenry. Regret at turning down the Southern Pacific proposal that the populace pay a $60,000 subsidy to bring the rail road to town spread through San Juan like wildfire. Businesses, offices and houses were boarded up and abandoned.

Some of the largest businesses were among the first to leave, many other businessmen and professionals followed, and their employees soon joined the exodus. Hollister offered greater prospects for growth; this was borne out by census figures. In 1870 Hollister had a population of two hundred, and in 1873 a special census showed a population of more than two thousand (some boosters claimed more like four thousand).

San Juan may have reached a peak population of one thousand to fifteen hundred in 1870-71, which dropped to 400, according to an unofficial 1872 census. The official census of San Juan in 1879 was 2,638, but this is misleading because the figure included almost everyone living in what later became San Benito County except those in the Hollister area.

By October, the town council settled down to more orderly meetings. In November the town mar-

shal resigned. The next month the cost of liquor licenses was reduced from five dollars to two dollars per quarter.

On February 21, 1872, the trustees instructed City Attorney R. H. Brotherton to sue all taxpayers who were delinquent in paying their taxes. Two months later the trustees voted to pay a new town marshal thirty dollars per month. A year earlier the marshal had turned in bills totaling sixty to seventy-five dollars monthly.

True to the council's past policy, the minutes of the meetings reported only the actual action taken, without a word as to why or why not.

Despite the loss of businesses and their employees, there was a core of people who remained to serve the prosperous farms of the area. Travelers still came through town, but their numbers slowly dwindled.

The second big disappointment for San Juan in this period of turmoil was the loss of the county seat.

The agitation previously mentioned for the formation of a new county gained momentum as the population grew. Filing the necessary papers for new homes, farms and businesses in Hollister required many hours or days of travel to the county seat, Monterey City.

At no time did the divisionists base their campaign on criticism of Monterey County. A new county on the east side of the mountains was simply a geographical necessity for the people.

The divisionists lost local elections but did get their petition placed before the state legislature. There were stumbling blocks there too, but they finally won passage of legislation for the new county. Governor Newton Booth signed the bill February 12, 1874, and San Benito County was created.

A commission was appointed to set up the organization of the county, the officers to be elected, the supervisorial districts defined, and other such de-

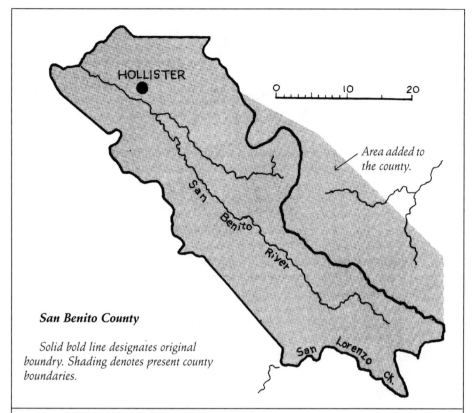

San Benito County

Solid bold line designates original boundry. Shading denotes present county boundaries.

Boundaries of San Benito County as in Owen Coy's definitive book, California County Boundaries, *of 1923, revised in 1980 by Valley Publishers. Note the New Idria area (shown outside the solid bold line) granted by Fresno County to San Benito County. Fresno County found it an expensive area to police, and San Benito County probably appreciated the added tax base in its own back-country.*

tails. The commissioners were Thomas S. Hawkins, Jess Whitton, Mark Pomery, John Breen, and H. M. Hays.

The commissioners met February 18, 1874, to organize the county. John Breen, who had been district attorney and judge of Monterey County, was elected chairman. He resigned the judgeship in Monterey County, and the governor appointed him judge in San Benito County until the next election. Breen won reelection with 1,026 votes, usually referred to as unanimous. He is shown on the records as the candidate of the Republican, Democratic and Workingmen parties in the general election. The records also show that thirteen votes were cast for R. H. Brotherton as an independent candidate, which may mean write-ins. Brotherton operated a drug store and was also an attorney in San Juan.

An election was called to elect the other county officers. Most were from the Hollister district.

Thomas Flint was elected supervisor from the San Juan district number two. He did not run for

reelection, but in 1880 was elected state senator from the three-county senatorial district composed of Monterey, Santa Cruz and San Benito counties.

The roster of the remainder of elected officials shows few other residents of San Juan in public office.

Hollister was named the county seat of San Benito County, which should not have surprised anyone. When the new county was first suggested, the planners from the Colonel Hollister group anticipated a struggle to take the seat of government away from San Juan. They made certain that the boundaries of the new county should not include some population centers west of San Juan that would have been supporters of San Juan. As it turned out, San Juan lost so many people in the exodus of 1871 that there would not have been enough votes to put up a good fight.

The loss of the county seat was in the long run more serious than the loss of the railroad. Be that as it may, old-timers in San Juan felt "robbed."

Neither the growth of the town nor the exodus in the fall of 1871 resulted in any great increase in crimes.

The mid-1870s, however, was the time the area's most famous outlaw and his gang chose to make a raid in southern San Benito County. The raid and the events that followed have been the subject of many books and magazine articles through the years.

Tiburcio Vasquez was born in Monterey. His ever-loyal lieutenant, Cleodovis Chaves, was from San Juan. Chaves attended San Juan schools and lived on the outskirts of town near where the Alameda met the Hollister road.

Vasquez made a statement after his capture in which he said he was born August 11, 1835, but by most accounts it was 1837. He also said he had a

SOUTHERN PACIFIC LOSES FRIENDS

By 1875 relations between the railroad and both farmers and businessmen had become tarnished. A publication named *Resources of San Benito County* with a Hollister dateline of June 1875 explained just how unhappy the local people were with the railroad. In a front page article about the railroad they reported:

"Besides this road [S.P.], a narrow gauge railroad is in contemplation from Hollister to some point on the ocean (Monterey or Santa Cruz or both). The company, which embraces some of the most substantial men in the county, has been incorporated and the first percentage of the capital stock paid in. . . . The stock has all been taken by the citizens of this section, who propose to control it in the interest of the people . . . farmers and merchants of San Benito County will have it in their power measurably to regulate the rates of freight, which heretofore, owing to the want of a competing line, have been too high. The projectors . . . mean business, and there is not the slightest doubt that the road will be built in 1876."

No further report of the project has been found, but it is quite obvious that no road was built.

—Microfilm—Bancroft Library

sister living in San Juan. Vasquez did not mention it, but from 1863 to 1870 his mother, Doña Guadalupe Cantua de Vasquez, operated a small Mexican restaurant called La Fonda Mexicana. It was located in an adobe building on Third Street, where in 1908 the Taix building was built. Quite possibly, Vasquez's sister continued to operate what has been called a tamale shop.

When he was fifteen, Vasquez was reported to have opened a dance hall in Monterey. He makes no mention of this, but in the statement he wrote, "I was in the habit of attending balls and parties given by native Californians, into which the Americans, then beginning to be numerous, would force themselves and shove native-born men aside, monopolizing the dance and the women." He continued on much the same theme.

Many other Mexicans were resentful of the loss of land and their status as a result of the war nearly twenty-five years earlier. Fortunately, most of them

found a better way to express their feelings than Tiburcio Vasquez. For several years he and his gang lived well from banditry along the Central Coast area.

Vasquez, Chaves and their fellow bandits avoided robbing or terrorizing the people of San Juan. They were often visitors here, and from most reports they were congenial and well-liked. Many have said they believed that Vasquez never killed anyone.

Vasquez and Chaves' final raid in Central California was only a few miles from San Juan. The gang attacked Snyder's store in Tres Pinos at about five o'clock, August 26, 1873.

Many detailed accounts have been published about the incident, but the bottom line was that three men were killed. Some witnesses placed blame for two of the deaths on Vasquez, but some writers have called this circumstantial, because there was much firing going on. Vasquez himself wrote that he and Chaves were late in arriving at the store and the shootings were contrary to his orders.

After gathering all the money, food and clothing that they wanted, the gang headed for Los Angeles.

"El Capitan Vasquez was quite a favorite with the señoritas," Vasquez wrote after his capture. This may have been uppermost in his mind because it is what led to his capture.

On the way to Los Angeles, Vasquez succeeded in seducing the wife of Adon (Don) Leiva, a longtime member of the gang. Leiva discovered them and rushed out, swearing revenge. He hurried to Los Angeles and made a deal with the sheriff to turn state's evidence against Vasquez.

Sheriff William R. Rowland made his plans carefully, and on May 15, 1874, a posse from his office was sent to a house "about ten miles due west of Los Angeles, toward Santa Monica, and not far from Cahuenga Pass."

The posse interrupted Vasquez's breakfast with a knock on the door. A woman answered the door, and deputies rushed in while Vasquez headed for the back door and his horse in a fusillade of bullets.

With only flesh wounds, he threw up his hands and said, "Boys, you have done well; I have been a damned fool but it is all my own fault. I'm done up."

Vasquez was held at the Los Angeles jail until his wounds healed, and was then taken to San Jose. San Benito County was just being formed and had no fa-

Tiburcio Vasquez

cilities for a major trial, so it was in San Jose that a jury found Vasquez guilty of murder. He was hanged in the courtyard of the San Jose jail on March 19, 1875. The sheriff sent out 400 invitations to the hanging, and a good response filled the courtyard.

Chaves swore vengeance for the hanging, but the state had offered a $2,500 reward for him, so he went south. A San Juan businessman, Louis Riggio, Jr., went after Chaves and caught up with him in New Mexico, where he killed him. To collect the reward, he cut off Chaves' head and brought it back in a gunny sack.

So ended one of the most notorious and colorful gangs in early California.

Affairs continued to slow down for San Juan, but the community was held together by a stable farm economy—and then came 1877, a dry year.

The dry year was most severe in the south, but farmers in the San Juan area were so hard hit that they could harvest only meager crops if any at all.

Prices fell and money tightened up so only small loans with liquid security were available at banks.

People from the south abandoned their parched farms and headed north looking for work or land with water. Many went through San Juan. Mylar tells how the wagons would pass by his farm, sometimes in a steady stream. He also wrote about local efforts to salvage a few dollars for food.

A butcher and Flint-Bixby and Company rented space for some large kettles, one for old hogs and the other for old sheep, to be slaughtered for hog feed. They hoped to save the more valuable young stock for another day when the weather had cooled and the rains returned. Sheep were valued at about fifty cents each.

A man who owned about two thousand goats killed some each day and then sold them by quarters. A hindquarter sold for thirty-five cents, a forequarter was somewhat less.

The farmers worked hard to avoid ruin from the drought and were rewarded by rains in the middle of January 1878, but the drought was not completely over. That year the fall was drier than usual so Mylar joined the exodus and with his wife and their year-old baby left for Astoria, Oregon.

There was no drought there! It rained, and rained, and rained. Mrs. Mylar had a miserable trip up on the steamship. She never wanted to see one again, but the overabundance of rains finally washed away her reluctance for another ocean voyage, and the family returned to San Juan.

For a town its size, San Juan had a nice selection of benevolent societies in the late 1870s.

San Juan's Masonic Lodge, Texas Lodge, No. 46, Free and Accepted Masons, was chartered in 1854 and built its lodge hall soon afterward on Second Street opposite the mission.

The Eastern Star, Ceanothus Chapter, No. 45, was organized in 1879 with Mary Ann Flint as worthy matron.

The San Benito Lodge No. 159, International Order of Odd Fellows (IOOF) was founded April 30, 1869. The lodge held its early meetings on Mondays in George Pullen's hall. In 1876 it moved to the Masonic Hall, where it continued meeting until 1901. It was to be nearly thirty years after its organization before the Odd Fellows lodge had a building of its own. In 1905 it bought a lot at Third and Polk streets for one hundred dollars. Two years later it bought a school building for $560 from the San Juan School District and moved the building to the lot at Third and Polk.

The *San Juan Argonaut* of October 6, 1880, gave details on other groups.

Mrs. E. L. Baker was a leader of the International Order of Good Templars (IOGT). The group

The Masonic Lodge building on Second Street was built in 1868-69 on a budget of $1,200.00. The Texas Lodge No. 46, F. & A.M., was organized in 1854 by twenty men who were mostly from Texas or other states in the south. They met in various places until the National Hotel was built in 1858 with a narrow room where they could meet. Membership had grown to more than one hundred when they decided to build their own building. Their first tenant was attorney R. H. Brotherton, who paid twelve and a half dollars per month. The lodge and building were destined to serve many functions in the community in the years to follow.

met Fridays in the Masonic Hall. Miss Julia Black was secretary of the San Juan Lodge No. 134.

The IOGT of San Juan was chartered in October 1870 with IOGT units from Salinas, Monterey and Castroville on hand to assist with the installation. Salinas Lodge provided a speaker, readings and music for dancing, which lasted long into the night. Dr. C. G. Cargill, M.D. was active in the group but was out of town at the time. He was an active citizen in many activities for several years.

The Reverend V. Closa was parish priest in 1880, and the Reverend L. H. Mead was pastor of the Congregational Church. The Reverend Mr. Holcum also preached there during this period.

This list of San Juan businesses in 1881 is difficult to compare with the 1870 list from the Gazette. The latter was an abbreviated list of only the larger stores.

The merchants of the town listed in the 1881 *History of San Benito County* were Joseph Bowie, F. A. Backer, M. Gardella, M. Filouchean, and B. Samit.

Dr. C. G. Cargill, a graduate in medicine of old Dartmouth University, was "proprietor of a drug store in connection with which he practices his profession with marked success." He was also postmaster and agent for Wells, Fargo & Company's express.

SAN JUAN'S OWN SOLDIER OF FORTUNE

William G. Walker wasn't born in San Juan but arrived there before he was nineteen. He was from Nashville, Tennessee, and was one of the Southerners who arrived in the early 1850s and applied for a charter for the Texas Lodge 46, F. & A. Masonic Lodge records tell of Walker's expeditions south of the border:

"The adventurer [Walker] in July, 1853, organized an expedition against Sonora, Mexico, and was compelled to surrender to the U.S. Command at San Diego.

"Two years later, Walker again became impatient with a staid life and went to Nicaragua with 62 followers, and, in conjunction with a small native force, defeated a Nicaraguan army of 540 men at Rivas. Walker was made secretary of war and commander of the army there. He established a government, but was later driven from power by the U.S. in May, 1857.

"Three years later he was again in the limelight when he invaded Honduras (1860) and was finally captured by the British and turned over to Honduras authorities. He wrote the book 'The War in Nicaragua' in that year before he was shot in Trujillo, Honduras on September 13, 1860. Incidentally, Walker demitted from Texas lodge on September 9, 1854."

Mark Regan operated the only local stage connection with the trains.

E. W. Bowman & Sons, blacksmiths, wheelwrights and skilled mechanics.

This etching of the mission from the 1882 History of San Benito County is one of the first to show the belltower added in 1876. The friar designed it so the lower part of the tower could be used as a reading room where he could check the punctual ringing of the bells.

J. R. Allen, blacksmith and horseshoer.

John Nagle, painter and paperhanger.

The Plaza Hotel, A. Camours.

The National Hotel, George Pullen.

John Anderson, tinsmith, stones and hardware.

Angelo Zanetta, livery stable.

J. G. Beuttler, brewery.

Victor Gerbet, vineyardist, winery and store or saloon on Second Street.

James Stanley, saddle and harness shop.

Jean Lacoste, bakery and fruit store.

C. Quersin, French restaurant.

At this time the San Juan School had about a hundred students with a staff of three: Mr. W. H. Housch, principal, and Miss Housch and Miss Pierpont, teachers.

The San Juan justice of the peace was John Golden, and constable was Jack Smith in 1881. William T. Brown was sheriff.

For a quiet farm center it would seem that San Juan had a very respectable variety and number of stores and organizations. It was to be several years before there would be many great changes.

Until the fourteen issues of San Juan Bautista newspapers were found on microfilm, the *San Juan Argonaut* was just the name of another short-lived newspaper, and it seemed a poor match with the newspapers of ten years earlier. Its format of only three columns on a smaller than usual page looked somewhat amateurish.

It had every right to be amateurish.

A look at the masthead raises the question of why it was "dedicated to the public schools and the community." The answer is in the next three lines of type. Frank Abbe, George Abbe, and Henry Sherwood, editors and publishers of the *Argonaut*, were all students at the local schools. This was issue No. 8 of the bimonthly paper, which would be terminated at the end of the school term.

With this in mind, it is fun reading, and the meeting notices are good insight into activities in the early 1880s. The editorial does not take sides but outlines the important issues in the presidential election to be held just a few days later. Incidentally, there are no political advertisements, even at twenty-five cents per inch.

As was then common practice, the front page is devoted to national or international news, notices and poetry.

Page two is filled with two full columns of local news items, of which none is more than eight lines, and only one that long.

Two hunters bagged three deer and a wildcat.

Charles Foster joined Good Templars.

Gregg Foster is renovating his residence.

There will be a meeting of the Garfield and Arthur Club tonight at 7 o'clock. [But what night is tonight?]

Patrick Breen had a cancer successfully removed from his lip.

There is a total of twenty-eight items, but the rest are not as interesting. Five ads appeared on page three.

The Annual Teachers Institute had been held in Hollister, and "all the teachers of the county, twenty-eight, were present." This report and a column of notes from Hollister take about a half of page four. The rest is devoted to a full column of "Miscellany," short happenings elsewhere, plus a report on the Good Templars' regional meeting.

Of the editors and publishers of the *Argonaut*, Frank and George Abbe were most active for over fifty years in community affairs. George served as mayor in the booming first years of the twentieth century, and Frank served as mayor for ten years before his death in 1932. Both were enthusiastic workers on the annual festival committee. The Abbe family came to San Juan in 1856, and members of the family were a positive influence on the town for more than one hundred years.

San Juan had its admirers, those who felt attracted by an appeal or aura that defied definition then, just as they do today.

One such admirer was author Helen Hunt Jackson, who came to San Juan to write a book that would do for the Indians what *Uncle Tom's Cabin* did for the Negroes. It was in the autumn of 1873 that this well known and admired writer came to San Juan.

Her book, which was later named *Ramona*, might have been written in San Juan except for the lack of housing and the clash of two women of different temperaments.

Mrs. Jackson's visit to San Juan was the subject of an article by Owen Treleven in the *Overland Monthly* of June 1916. It was reprinted in the *Mission News* of July 5.

When Mrs. Jackson arrived at Sargent Station "she boarded the stage of Mark Regan—than whom there is no more picturesque character in all of California."

Regan took her to the Plaza Hotel, but that did not offer the desired atmosphere. Father Close did not think the mission rooms were suitable for Mrs. Jackson and her sister, Annie Fiske.

The next place Regan showed them was the Castro-Breen adobe. Treleven tells of that unfortunate meeting:

> Mrs. Jackson, after a cursory survey of the picturesque exterior, expressed an emphatic desire to occupy the place with her secretary, if the caretaker would accept accommodations at Mrs. Jackson's expense in the Plaza Hotel. Accordingly they knocked at the door.
>
> The house at that time was in the charge of a woman whose brogue might without great difficulty be attributed to a nativity in the Emerald Isle. She had been equally blessed with hair of a fiery hue, and the temperament that is generally thought to accompany its possession, and children of all ages and sizes.
>
> On her way to the door to answer the summons, the woman stumbled over one of the numerous progeny who was engaged in the delightful occupation of dipping both hands in a molasses jar and transferring a portion of the contents to his mouth, clothing and surroundings in general. The woman caught the child up—astride her hip—and objecting strenuously to his removal from the source of so much sweetness, the youngster immediately began to claw his mother's hair and clothing, and the sticky ludicrous spectacle presented to the visitors on the door being opened was too much for Mrs. Jackson's sense of humor, she was convulsed with laughter.
>
> The woman stood there glowering at those who were 'makin' fun o' her darlin'' until the proposition was put to her to allow Mrs. Jackson to occupy the dwelling, when she replied most emphatically that they and 'the likes' of them would gain entrance only 'over my dead body,' and so Mrs. Jackson was forced to abandon the project and seek another locality for the writing of *Ramona*.

Although the book was not written in San Juan, Mrs. Jackson was deeply impressed by the town and

JIM JACK, THE MUSTARD KING

Jim Jack, "The big-hearted Chinaman"

About 1880 San Juan was blessed with a philanthropist whose generosity lightened burdens for hundreds, possibly thousands if the children he gave candies to are included, for more than forty years.

His name was Jim Jack, or to some China Jack and, to others the Mustard King. Through the years he was Jim Jack to most. No real name was ever known, or most certainly ever recorded.

Jim Jack, who as an Oriental could not own property, gave $3,500 to Charles and Peter Clausen to buy twenty-six acres southeast of San Juan. He only asked of them that he be allowed to live on a corner of the land. The cabin he lived in long stood on Mission Vineyard road. It measured twelve by twelve feet.

There are two good accounts of his life.

In 1919 the *San Francisco Chronicle* sent a reporter to San Juan to learn about Jim Jack, who had recently passed through that city. The report was reprinted in the *San Juan Mission News* of June 21, 1919. The reporter wrote:

"Jim Jack came to California fifty-two years ago (1867) when he was sixteen years old, and obtained a job on the Tom Flint ranch, near San Juan, poisoning the squirrels. In 1879 he stepped into prominence overnight.

"The year previous there had been a heavy rainfall and the wild mustard had overgrown the crops, so he promised to clean the land if the farmers would give him the mustard seed. With one hundred other Chinese, he cleaned up 10,000 acres that netted him $40,000 when sold to French mustard manufacturers.

"In 1879 there was a drought and much suffering among the farmers of the San Benito valley, so Jim Jack gave away $20,000 that year, helping everybody. Provisions of every description by the ton, hay and barley were hauled from San Francisco and distributed around. He provisioned some people to run a year, saw that their stock had feed, provided others with cattle and horses and paid doctor bills.

"By 1880 Jim Jack had discovered the road to happiness and ever since he has made it a practice to smooth the way for hundreds of people.

JIM JACK'S CABIN
JIM JACK WAS KNOWN AS CHINA JIM,
THE MUSTARD KING. IN THE 1880'S HE
GATHERED MUSTARD SEED FROM THE
GRAIN FIELDS IN THE SAN JUAN VAL-
LEY. JIM JACK, "THE BIG-HEARTED
CHINAMAN" HAD "THAT RAREST OF GIFTS,
THE GIFT OF GIVING.
MONTEREY VIEJO CHAPTER
E CLAMPUS VITUS
NOV. 17, 1973

"Of late years he has been running a truck garden under the shadow of the huge cross planted on the Gabilan mountains, by the San Juan Mission padres, and he has been applying the doctrine, 'Tis more blessed to give than to receive.'

"To those who were shy of funds but too proud to take charity, he always managed to slip a sack of potatoes and sacks of vegetables when they were not at home. Likewise he had an eye for the widow or the expectant mother of a poor household, and out of the clear sky would come a generous supply of milk and groceries, or dress goods to last for months.

"Although he was always liberal at Christmas, he never forgot that there were 364 other days when cupboards were lightly stocked and stockings empty. Nor did he confine himself to necessaries. Always with the flour and bacon went candy, cookies and oranges, for as he maintained, 'Bread allightie but cookie make slunsline in the face.' At his little shack he had boxes of oranges, fruits and sweetmeats and the wellworn trail to his door proved their lure to the children of San Juan.

"At one time Jim Jack was asked why he persisted in giving away all he made, especially after he had worked so hard to get it. His answer was typical of the man, 'No catchee children, so why leavem money for Billie Black?' Black at that time was Public Administrator of San Benito county.

"In all this humble Chinese charitable acts he insisted on being in the background. He obtained his plea-

sures in giving, and he did not want to be present when his gifts arrived, as he said it was embarrassing to all concerned.

"There will be much sadness this coming Christmas in San Benito, for Jim Jack, the man who played the part of Santa Claus so well, has gone, never to return."

The second source of information is from Mylar, who called Jim Jack a "most generous and well-liked man by children and families in need."

Mylar offered no dates and did not tell of any $40,000 year. He says Jim Jack continued through the years to gather the mustard seed from the cleaners on the grain harvesters. In other fields where the mustard choked out everything else, Jim Jack would hire other Chinese to cut the mustard and they would flail the seeds out on a canvas. All was later cleaned for the market.

Jim Jack lived about midway between San Juan and Hollister. Mylar tells of his personal knowledge of Jim Jack:

"He always drove a little one-horse cart, and in the front, at his feet, he carried a good-sized box in which he had candy in little bags, oranges and sweet cookies in small cartons. These he gave to the children on his trips to Hollister or San Juan. I have known of him hiring a four-horse team and driver to take him to Hollister at which town he bought flour for a load, had it driven back to San Juan and distributed among the laboring men's families. On another occasion he bought three hundred sacks of potatoes all of which he gave away. He also kept a few hens, the eggs he would take to the store and sell, receiving a credit slip for the sale. These slips he would give to the families whom he thought needed something out of the store. No one ever knew how much money he had, unless it was a banker. I heard him say that he gave away all the interest on his money. When I was with a threshing outfit I would spread a sheet behind the cleaner for him. Every year, a day or two before Thanksgiving, he would drive up the avenue and give my wife several packages of mincemeat, raisins, candies, and nuts. To the children he would give fifty cents or a dollar each, and before he left he would get close to me and slip a dollar in my pocket and whisper, 'You get a cup of beer.'

"Jim Jack's visit to San Francisco was when he was going back to his homeland. The *Mission News* reported January 3, 1920, 'Jim Jack Dies in His Native Land.'"

That is why he returned home.

Dr. Charles C. Cargill, physician and assemblyman

Cargill's Brass Band in 1890. The band played during the holidays of 1870-71 and for many years after. He is on the far left with his horn. At the far right is the drummer, CC Zanetta, town constable.

wrote some scenes about the mission and town in her book. Over thirty thousand copies of *Ramona* were sold before her death in 1885.

Mrs. Jackson loved the mission and town but later wrote a rather bleak report of San Juan in 1883:

**San Juan Bautista of 1883—A Tribute
By Helen Hunt Jackson**

Glimpses of California and the Missions
Why the little town of San Juan Bautista continues to exist is a marvel. It is shut out and cut off from everything; only two or three hundred souls are left in it; its streets are grass-grown; half its houses are empty. But it has a charm of sun, valley, hill and seaward off-look unsurpassed in all California.

At San Juan Bautista there lingers more of the atmosphere of the olden time than is to be found in any other place in California. The Mission church is well preserved; its grounds are enclosed and cared for; in its garden are still blooming roses and vines, in the shelter

of palms, and with the old stone sundial to tell time. In the sacristy are oak chests, full of gorgeous vestments of brocades, with silver and gold laces. On one of these robes is an interesting relic. A lost or worn out silver tassel had been replaced by patient Indian workers with one of fine shredded rawhide; the shreds wound with silver wire, and twisted into tiny rosettes and loops, closely imitating the silver device.

The church fronts south, on a little green-locust walled plaza—the sleepiest, sunniest, dreamiest place in the world. To the east the land falls off abruptly, so that the palling [fence] on that side of the plaza is outlined against the sky, and its little locked gate looks as if it would open into the heavens. The mission buildings used to surround this plaza; after the friars' day came rich men living there; and a charming inn is now kept in one of their old adobe houses. On the east side of the church is a succession of three terraces leading down to a valley. On the upper one is the old graveyard, in which it is said there are sleeping four thousand Indians.

In 1825 there were spoken at this mission thirteen different Indian dialects.

Just behind the church is an orphan girls' school, kept by the Sisters of the Sacred Heart. At six o'clock every morning the bells of the church ring for mass as they used to ring when over a thousand Indians flocked at the summons. Today, at the sound, there comes a procession of little girls and young maidens, the black-robed sisters walking before them with crossed hands and placid faces. One or two Mexican women, with shawls over their heads, steal across the faint paths of the plaza and enter the church.

I shall always recollect the morning when I went too. The silence of the plaza was in itself a memorial service, with locust blossoms a-winging incense. It was barely dawn in the church as the shrill yet sweet childish voices lifted up the strains of the Kyrie Eleison. I seemed to see the face of Father Junipero in the dim lighted chancel, and the benediction was as solemn as if he himself had spoken it.

The town continued the usual routine during the late 1880s. There appeared to be some problems of collecting taxes one year, but when the town's trustees got the final accounting from the deputy marshal everything was found in order.

Hay and grains were major crops in the nineteenth century and horses and oxen were the motive power. Things were due to change to more varied crops and railroads, trucks and automobiles were to become the norm.

In 1888 citizens complained of too many cattle in the streets. The marshal was ordered to clear the streets of the cattle and also of thistles. He was authorized to pay two dollars per day to whoever did the latter. Repair work on the Alameda wasn't done because of the trustees' failure to get a bid. All was fine until 1889. Citizens who didn't like the trustees' order to keep cattle off the streets petitioned for livestock to be allowed to run at large. The petition was rejected on a three-to-one vote. This was underscored by instruction to the marshal to clean the streets and keep them clean.

The 1880s were otherwise uneventful, maybe dreary as we look at them now, but the residents then had their activities, as we have seen.

The farm economy was fairly stable, but in 1893 a depression swept the entire country that made things difficult here as elsewhere. There was a great shortage of money. Banks would lend money only on the most fluid and marketable collateral. San Juan was probably able to avoid some of the suffering because the farms were mostly self-supporting.

A partnership identified only as Gates & Baptist may have had a glimmer of hope for improvement in the town in 1893. Although the *San Juan Enterprise* was not included in a list of newspapers later prepared by Ed Lamb, the last editor of the *San Juan Mission News*, another publication said that the partners started a newspaper by that name in 1893. This may have been an effort to enlarge the coverage of the *Hollister Enterprise* in this period of national depression.

Of greater importance, the town was touched that year by a wondrous and mysterious invention, the telephone. True, only one telephone was installed, and that was a public phone in Dr. Cargill's drug store, but the town was destined for more.

The Sunset Telephone Company was expanding south and east of San Francisco. Its next new line from Gilroy was going to be to the Monterey area. The company planned to route it through Hollister until perennial booster Mark Regan pointed out to Sunset that it could save several miles by coming through San Juan.

From this point it was only weeks before Sunset started its eastern extension from San Juan to the company's Central California network via Panoche Pass, Whitesbridge and Fresno. It must have been a thrill for the drifting town to have construction crews working on this marvelous invention here.

In addition, their plans were reported in big city newspapers as having originated in San Juan.

The next line out of San Juan was to Lompoc, which was to be a connection point with Los Angeles. Imagine talking from San Juan with someone in San Francisco or even Los Angeles!

Cargill's drug store was a natural location for the telephone office, because it was already the telegraph service center. When the local switchboard was installed in 1900 it had acquired ten more customers. The equipment was the manual hand-crank system, and calls could be cleared through the switchboard only during the day while the store was open. If you didn't say all you wanted to say by 9:00 P.M. it had to wait for morning. Service grew and improved, but the old equipment was used until 1957.

The Sunset Company later became a unit of Pacific Telephone and Telegraph.

Father Engelhardt wrote that the community's celebration of the 100th anniversary of the founding of the San Juan Bautista Mission had been cancelled. He apparently had been misinformed.

Dorothy Flint tells just how it was in her memoirs, *Escarpment on the San Andreas*:

On June 24, 1897, the centennial of the founding of the Mission San Juan Bautista had been celebrated in San Juan with appropriate rites in the mission church and with a full day and evening of other commemorative events. Included were an open air 'literary program' staged against the venerable backdrop of the mission corridor itself, a long historical parade depicting various aspects of the hundred-year period under three flags, a 'sold-out' barbecue,

an early-evening band concert, and a climactic grand ball in the widely famed Plaza Hall. With their senator-son as master of ceremonies and grand marshal, their younger son as one of his aides, and their new daughter-in-law as a tireless photographer, the aging pioneers of the Rancho San Justo had participated wholeheartedly in the historic occasion.

Considerable planning went into the observance, as evidenced by the souvenir program. There was an ample amount of advertising by local businesses.

The editors of the program did a considerable amount of research to glean the following "firsts" in the hundred-year history of the mission:

The principal record books of Mission San Juan Bautista are seven in number, three of baptism, two of burials, and two of marriages,

This souvenir program for the Centennial Celebration on June 24, 1897 is in the San Juan Library. The introduction reads: "Oh, these Missions! These old Spanish Missions with their towers and their crosses and their bells — deep-toned, yet sweet, as they fill the quiet Sabbath morn with their melody — these were a part of our earliest recollections. And now, whether proudly adorning a commanding slope, or nestling in a quiet vale, or lying in ruins on some desolate plane, there arises that sympathy of heart and soul on beholding one of these old Spanish Missions." An inside page reads: "By Frank B. Abbe and Nellie Duncan Gleason, with drawings by Joe D. Gleason."

and from them may be gathered the following facts: Up to June 24, 1897, there had been twelve thousand one hundred and eighty baptisms, four thousand five hundred and fifty-seven burials, and nineteen hundred marriages.

The first baptism was Juan Bautista, tribe of Absayme, July 11, 1797, by Fr. Martinez. There were two other baptisms on this day.

The first white baptism was Francisco Ballesteros, Aug. 22, 1797. Francisco Ballesteros was also the first burial, recorded Sept. 23, 1797. Born Aug. 21, 1797. The father, Juan de José Ballesteros, was an officer at the garrison, the mother was Teresa.

The first marriage took place Oct. 5, 1797. The contracting parties were Matheo Armmex and Manuela Nocnoc, neophytes, the former of the tribe of Frutca, and the latter of the tribe of Aicee.

The first white marriage occurred Nov. 4, 1805, between Joaquin Buelna and Maria Guadalupa Rodiguez, by Fr. Domingo Furrate.

It is a strange fact that the padres leave no records of historical value. Here and there are found meager marginal notes respecting the mission or an event in the life of a padre.

The upper photos show Ernest "CC" Zanetta as a young man and again in 1936. The lower photo is dated 1890. CC is in the driver's seat of his elegant Victorian carriage and Henry Regan is in the passenger seat.

As we turn from the nineteenth century to the twentieth century, it is appropriate to recognize a San Juan man who worked as a lawman in both eras. Ernest "CC" Zanetta served the town well for sixty-six years, from 1879 to 1945.

He was the first constable of the San Juan Township and chief of police of San Juan Bautista, an office he held when he died at the age of eighty-seven. Zanetta was the oldest active peace officer in California at that time in point of years of service and age.

The son of Angelo Zanetta of Plaza Hotel fame, CC began his career in 1879 when he became a deputy sheriff of San Benito County. He then won an elec-

A social group of local young women at the end of the century. They are identified by Carrol L. Haro as: left to right, top row: Lotte Regan Burnett, Minnie Pearce Patterson, Belle D. Black; middle row: Jesse Bigley Hallaran, unknown; bottom row: Tot Smith Moore and Iris K. Flint.

Photo: Flint Collection

tion to the post of constable of the San Juan Judicial District. He was reelected twice, but in 1888 he was unseated under a rather strange voting procedure.

Constable candidates were voted on independently, but they had to run and be elected as two-man teams. Zanetta and his partner ended up with the low vote in 1888 and during the next two years he remained active as a deputy sheriff. Two years later, with a new partner, he won the election and continued to win for fifty-five more years. Just before the turn of the century, in 1898, Zanetta won reelection by a vote of 178 to 49. This has been cited as typical of his usual majority.

CC had an extraordinary memory. Newspapers regularly carried news of his remembering and identifying wanted criminals as they passed through the highway town of San Juan. As capturer, he often shared his capture of the culprit with officers in nearby towns. He also participated in man hunts in

the nearby mountains, and each incident created a story of its own.

Zanetta often remarked that he had seen San Juan through periods of high prosperity and through days of deep depression when residents moved away by the hundreds, leaving little more than a ghost city: "Only a handful of residents remained in town."

How did Ernest Zanetta become CC instead of E.Z. or something else? One story is that he was called Charlie when young and that in some contorted way it was changed to the nickname of CC. The other story was that he was called Sissy, and that was shortened to CC.

The latter seems unlikely, as he was involved in many sports as well as being active in training programs for the volunteer fire department. He had a straightforward attitude and was a drummer in the San Juan Brass Band. He enjoyed music and dancing as well as basketball and wrestling, hardly activities that might have led to the nickname Sissy.

Whatever the reason, CC it was, and the residents of San Juan respected and admired him for all of his sixty-six years as a peace officer.

Schools of San Juan

We are fortunate that pictures of the schools of San Juan exist to show us the changes through the years. In the early years smaller schools were built near the students, as transportation improved, and students could travel larger schools were built.

"The cornerstone of our splendid new San Juan Grammar School was laid Saturday afternoon, June 4, 1927, with appropriate and impressive ceremonies." (*San Juan Mission News* of June 10, 1927)

In true San Juan tradition, some of the work on the school was contributed. The morning of the dedication "energetic citizens volunteered their services and with tractors, scrapers and teams leveled the land around the building. At noon ladies of the Parent-Teacher Association served a hot lunch of meat loaf, macaroni, beans and coffee."

Two hours later the cornerstone ceremonies began. In the evening the new auditorium filled to capacity for a dedication program. The school principal, school board members and some people involved in the construction all participated in the ceremonies. The school orchestra offered a number and students presented an entertainment program, all of which was praised by the newspaper.

The eighth grade class was to graduate the following Thursday. There were fourteen students in the class, indicating the school enrollment was well over one hundred at that time.

Another do-it-yourself story was about the students in a parade through town. Some schools might provide buses, but San Juan had the students gather all their belongings, books and equipment at the old school on the hill west of the mission and, carrying everything, walk down through town single file to the new school.

San Juan school district maintained a high school for more than twenty-five years, but in 1932 it was closed "because of the high cost per pupil for education." The school was operating as a branch of Hollister High School and offered only the first two years of high school.

They were proud of getting out a last yearbook, *El Gabilan*, on June 3, 1932. The cover was described as being very impressive. It showed Fremont Peak, the cross on the hill, and the outline of the town's rooftops and mission. The material was mimeographed by members of the class.

The last day of school was June 17. The day was celebrated with a trip to the beaches of Santa Cruz. The following year all high school students were bussed to Hollister.

San Juan Grammar School was built near Second Street in the northwest corner of town in 1868. This picture is believed to have been taken two years later, but it might have been any time up to 1907, when the building was sold to the IOOF Lodge and moved to Third and Polk streets, where it still stands.

Education remained important to the parents in San Juan, but at the end of the century some changes were due. The one-room schools like the one at right in San Juan Canyon became less common as transportation and roads improved. This building appears much better than many rural schools of the day.

A first-grade class in San Juan in 1896. Unfortunately, the only student identified is Achille (Bud) Callichotte, fourth from the left in the back row.

The graduating class of 1900 from San Juan High School. Left to right, Cora Mylar, Clerence McKee, Rosoline Kemp, Rupe (no other name given), an unidentified girl, and John Doughearty. The spellings of the names are as written on the back of the photo.

The San Juan Grammer School was built near First Street to the north of the mission land and west of the community center in 1907. This building replaced the two-story school building built in 1868 which was sold to the Odd Fellows Lodge.

The building to the right replaced the1907 building above when it was demolished in 1925-26. Joseph W. Cullumber helped his father demolish the building for salvage value. Much of the salvaged material ended up in the Cullumber family home. Both buildings were at the same location.

A New Century
A New Outlook

The beginning of the twentieth century was a decade-long event in San Juan Bautista.

The first ray of greater hope for the new century may have been in 1898, when the town again had a newspaper of its own. The publisher was H. G. Copeland, a printer who chose to name his newspaper the *San Juan Valley Echo*, the name used by one of the last papers in 1871. Before the end of the decade there would be two newspapers in the town.

Although limited in size, an interesting evidence of mercantile growth around the turn of the century is found in the number of San Juan business partnerships registered in the San Benito County clerk's office.

In 1874 there were two: John R. Comfort and Angelo Zanetta, operating a hotel and livery service, and the general merchandise store of Mathew Filousheau and Theophile Vache.

It was twenty-two years before another partnership was filed. On December 14, 1896, Frank B. Abbe and George C. Abbe filed as the Abbe Company, a general merchandise store.

The first Abbes arrived in San Juan in the mid-1850s so the partners were not new to the community, but the filing undoubtedly was evidence of a new aggressive stance. Frank and George will be remembered as the publishers of the *San Juan Argonaut* in 1880 while they were still in school.

The Abbe Company prospered and the family was active in innumerable civic and social events for many years. Frank B. Abbe served ten years as mayor and organized many parades for festivals and pageants. George was mayor in the first decade, was a director of the first bank, and had a leading role in the festivals, the volunteer fire department, and similar projects that spark a small town. It can prob-

ably be said that up to the 1930s either Frank or George was active in every important undertaking in San Juan.

On October 23, 1901, Arthur S. Moore and Irwin W. Moore filed as partners operating Moore Brothers, a general merchandise store that remained in business several years.

Another store opened in another five years. It was destined to remain in continuous operation for more than eighty-seven years. In 1906 Joe Cravea opened a shoe and clothing store which was passed on to his son, John, who operated it as John Cravea Clothing until at least 1994, when poor health forced him to retire.

The third partnership announced in this era was Pick Hardware Company. The partners were Fred N. Abbe and Edward R. Pearce. In future years Pearce served the community in many ways including as town trustee and San Benito County supervisor. As a young man he was an enthusiastic member of the volunteer fire department. The filing was dated April 6, 1910.

Three filings of partnerships in a little over ten years after twenty-two years of no activity must be indicative of the general rebirth of the town.

As has been reported already, the name of the town was changed in the middle of the decade. San Juan became San Juan Bautista as authorized by the U.S. Postal Department on November 16, 1905.

The town trustees were busy keeping up with innovative public services to bring a better lifestyle to the townspeople.

At the beginning of the twentieth century, San Juan had telephones—well, at least one telephone. The town had street lights and hired lamplighters to tend them.

A gas plant was operating in 1903, which undoubtedly kept the lamps lighted.

A franchise was issued in 1907 to Davenport Light and Power to supply electricity to the town. Davenport was a town north of Santa Cruz which, like San Juan, had limestone deposits for cement, so there was probably a connection with other shared interests. In any event the alliance was short-lived.

In less than two years, on April 6, 1909, a franchise for a street railroad and electricity in the city was signed with San Benito Light and Power Company. This later passed on to the Coast Counties Gas and Electric, Coast Valley Gas and Electric, and then to the Pacific Gas and Electric Company.

The town trustees decided to keep the town's water service under local control. Formation of a municipal waterworks was started June 5, 1908, by a three-to-two vote by the town trustees, at an estimated cost to the city of $12,000.

A special election was set for the townspeople to vote on a $12,000 bond issue. The voters enthusiastically supported the project on August 24 by a vote of eighty-six to six for the bond issue. That was a fourteen-to-one all-male vote—the opposition apparently stayed home. There was one blank vote.

The city set about ordering material for the new service, and bills came in to be paid from the bond fund. There were no city managers in those days, but many people lent their talents to small town projects, and this was especially true in San Juan Bautista.

The new water system was obviously planned, constructed, and managed by the trustees and their friends. Water sources have been changed and the waterworks modernized. The central plant was moved twice, but after nearly one hundred years it continues to serve the town well.

There is no positive record of when or for how long the two newspapers of the first decade were published.

H. G. Copeland and his *San Juan Valley Echo* were paid numerous times between 1901 and 1904 for both printing and legal advertising.

In June 1904 A. B. Shaw and the *San Juan Star* were paid for advertising and office supplies. There were quotes from the *Star* in the *Catholic Monitor* of San Francisco in 1907 but little more is known about this publication.

The *Echo* continued billings in 1905, and other reports say they published until 1911. When a legal

The Mission was severely damaged in the San Francisco earthquake of 1906. Restoration would require nearly fifty years.

notice was needed in 1909 the town's trustees ordered it placed in both papers.

Unfortunately, very few copies of the *Echo* or the *Star* have been found, but it appears certain that both of them were published for ten to twelve years in the early years of the twentieth century.

FROM OUT OF THE RUINS

The tragic San Francisco earthquake of April 1906 did severe damage to the mission church and some small adobe buildings in San Juan Bautista, but frame houses suffered little damage. Indirectly, the earthquake resulted in major changes in the town, both spiritually and economically.

The earthquake so severely wrecked decaying timbers in the mission that tiles were broken and solid adobe walls were cracked. A gigantic crack was opened in the central nave of the church. Father Closa decided that a small wooden church should be built as there were not enough funds to repair the damage.

The townspeople did not want to lose their mission and church. Early in 1907 public-spirited citizens of San Juan formed a committee which resolved to have a fiesta to raise money for repairs. The date was set for June 24, to commemorate the 110th anniversary of the founding of the mission.

Included in the plans was the purchase of a huge cross to replace the one destroyed on Mount Holy Cross. The dedication of the cross was attended by local dignitaries in company with Father Engelhardt, who blessed the cross. He came from Watsonville, where he was serving at Boys Orphanage.

The party left for the Mount Holy Cross by auto immediately after Mass and returned in time for the big parade. In its report of the event, San Francisco's *Catholic Monitor* attributed many of the details to the *San Juan Star* and the *San Juan Valley Echo*.

The floats in the parade were judged and first prize went to a representation of the arrival in San Juan of the first missionary. Surrounded by Indians, he was dressed in Franciscan garb and sandals and was holding a cross.

The parade ended at Taix's Park, where a band and choir presented a musical program which was interspersed by several speakers.

The afternoon was devoted to a series of races—horses, men, bicycles, and a potato race. Then thirty young women took over for a maypole dance, which "was carried out without a mistake." In the evening there was a grand ball in the Plaza Room.

All of this was quite traditional, and apparently the day was a financial success, arousing the citizens of San Juan as they had not been aroused for many years. But a major measure of its success was the support that was generated among people outside of town.

Prominent among these supporters were Mr. and Mrs. Fremont Older of San Francisco. Mr. Older was editor of the *San Francisco Bulletin* and Mrs. Older was the author of a popular book, *California Missions and Their Romance*.

In order to help raise the $18,000 (a huge amount then) needed to rehabilitate the mission, Mr. Older started plans for an even bigger fiesta in 1908. It would be specifically to raise the needed funds. He "not only started the project, but devoted time and energy to interesting hundreds of his friends, in short, insuring the success of the affair."

Reflecting the enthusiasm of Mr. and Mrs. Older, the 1908 event was called the Grand Spanish Fiesta and was scheduled for Saturday, October 31 and Sunday, November 1.

News reports reflect its success: "The village was crowded with strangers, hundreds of visitors coming from San Francisco, Oakland, San Jose, and other

Early in this century a state landmarks group began to mark the El Camino Real with Mission Bell signposts. In 1908, at its annual meeting, the Grand Parlor of the Native Daughters of the Golden West endorsed the project. Pictured here is a later signpost placed in front of the mission after the state AAA joined the project. A marksman put the 9 out of "1797."

cities, while the neighboring towns near San Juan practically turned out en masse for the event."

The fiesta began when the "white squadron of cars arrived from San Francisco led by the Olders' white Stanley Steamer." This was an impressive sight which had never before been seen in San Juan.

The official Saturday program started at eight o'clock in the evening with a "Grand Concert," followed at ten o'clock by a benefit ball and at midnight by a Spanish supper.

At nine o'clock Sunday morning the fiesta began with a baseball game between Salinas and San Juan teams which the local team won by a 6-to-3 score.

A special Mass began at 10:45 A.M. on the plaza east of the church and overlooking the San Benito Valley. Following was a barbecue of two steers in the olive orchard.

The official program listed an afternoon agenda beginning at 1:30 and consisting of vaquero races in full rig, Virginia Reel on horseback by cowboys and

THE CROSS ON PAGAN HILL:

On an evening, look to the southeast of San Juan and on the top of a treeless hill you will see a well lit cross. You can see it in the daytime, but it is not as well defined.

The story of the cross goes back to nearly the founding of the mission. Not the lighting, of course; it is a contribution of a town that has been dedicated to the maintenance of this historic marker.

It is believed to have been first built before 1803 when the padres became disturbed by the dedication of the Indians to the hill, which had been sacred to their forefathers. The pagans of the surrounding country would assemble on the hill, claiming that a spirit appeared and conversed with them at that spot. Very probably this prevented numbers of them from embracing the Gospel preached by the Franciscans.

The padres sought to enlighten the Indians without offending them by means which had proved effective in Mexico. A large cross was constructed and placed on the hill, and the visits of the spirit ceased. The missionaries were pleased with the results and on special occasions would take groups of converts to the cross for a special blessing.

Circumstances changed but the cross remained for about fifty years. Then a vandal or farmer in need of a gate post chopped it down. A short stump remained, but if seen by a hunter or hiker it had no meaning. It was about another fifty years before the townspeople became aware of the story of the cross on the hill.

They planned for nearly a year to replace the cross as a special feature of the 1907 fiesta celebrating the 110th anniversary of the founding of the mission. A committee composed entirely of non-Catholics collected means for construction and replacement of the cross.

Accordingly, on Monday, June 24 while Father Closa celebrated holy mass for people in a temporary chapel (because of the damage caused by the 1906 earthquake), the Rev. Fr. Zephyrin Engelhardt of the Boys' Orphanage in Watsonville set our for the hill. He was accompanied by Mr. and Mrs. George Moore, George Abbe and

A group visits the redwood cross on Pagan Hill in 1908.

Harry Breen. At the top of the hill Fr. Engelhardt, wearing his habit, blessed the memorial cross. The little group then hastened back to town in time for the festival parade.

This new cross on the hill was constructed of redwood, supplied by a man from the Watsonville area identified only as Mr. Haynes, according to Tony Taix. It stood twenty feet tall with an added six feet buried in a concrete base. The cross beam was sixteen feet, and both timbers were fourteen by fourteen inches

girls, hurdle jumping, fancy riding, steer-lassoing and tying, steer-riding, vaquero equipment races, relay race, bronco-lassoing and busting, etc.

San Juan won more than a baseball game that day. It won the rehabilitation of the mission. It won widespread recognition as a town as well as a big,

attractive mission. It won a rejuvenated leadership after being in the doldrums for more than thirty years.

San Juan Bautista received national recognition in the popular *Overland Monthly*. The article, "La Fiesta de San Juan Bautista," reported the event in detail by Thalia Weed Newcomb in Vol. 74,

A HERITAGE FROM EARLY MISSION DAYS

Four youths stand beside the new concrete cross in 1931.

The cross today.

wide. The cross weighed 3,000 pounds and required a six-horse team to take it up the hill.

In 1929, townspeople and the local cement plant cooperated to produce yet another cross when the redwood one was burned down. The huge cement cross is twenty-nine feet high, with nineteen-foot cross arms. There are no public roads leading to it, and it stands on private property. The San Juan Bautista Parlor No. 179

of the Native Daughters of the Golden West played a major role in starting the replacement project. They soon received cooperation and support from the recently organized San Juan Service Club, composed of local merchants and individuals. Both organizations supplied money as well as volunteer help to the effort.

The Pacific Portland Cement Company supplied the concrete for the cross. The company's superintendent, Frank F. Parker, was chairman of the total community committee.

The present cross is usually referred to as the 1929 replacement, but a progress report in the December 6, 1930 edition of the San Juan *Mission News* indicated considerable work remained to be done.

The news story was headed up as a progress report, and Mr. Parker reported that they had considerable trouble getting to the construction site. They had to make a road up to the top of the hill and then only light trucks were able to carry the material up.

In recent years the eighty-eight light globes on the 1929 cement cross have been removed. The cross is lit by a panel of spotlights. It is hoped that the new lighting will not provide targets as appealing as the globes were to irresponsible "hunters."

January 1909. Details included a report of the damage to the mission by the earthquake as well as the calls for assistance to save the mission. Publicity like this must have sparked even greater enthusiasm as the *Overland Monthly* had a large national distribution.

The mission reconstruction fund was supported by another series of June fiestas. The series began in 1912 with a celebration on Pentecost, sponsored by the I.D.E.S. Council No. 99, a Portuguese organization.

It was a two-day event beginning on Saturday with a parade to the picnic grounds and the crowning of the queen. In the evening there was a grand ball.

On Sunday, the people went as a unit to church, where the sermon was delivered in both Portuguese and English. The church service was followed by a play, a barbecue and a program. In the mid-1920s, the event was combined with the celebration of the Hollister I.D.E.S.

The festivals of the first decade financed the repairs of the major damage to the church, but many more festivals were required to complete restoration.

San Juan Bautista became known as the Festival Town. People continued to rally around to support the celebration of the founding of the mission on the weekend nearest June 24.

The festivals were usually a two-day event with a program that was fairly consistent. A parade through town, even on Third Street, which was Highway 101 until 1932, was the usual opening event. A barbecue on the mission grounds was traditional, and then there

Program   Oct. 31st and Nov. 1st

Grand Spanish Fiesta

San Juan, Cal.

1908

This handsome program was tied with a ribbon. It was subsidized by local merchants including Richard H. Flint (San Justo Dairy), Lavagnino Bros. whose ad reads "Dealers in Gent's Furnishing Goods, Boots and Shoes" and E. A. Pearce and Fred N. Abbe of Pick Hardware Co.

The dedication reads, "An appeal is made for the preservation of the venerable pile of brick and adobe, which withstanding the ravages of the elements for more than a century, was partially demolished in a few seconds of time on the fateful morn of April 18, 1906, and now no more is heard the chant of priest nor refrain of choir within the crumbling walls.

Unless immediate steps are taken to protect the walls, now laid bare to the winter rains, irreparable damage will be wrought and it will be but a matter of a few years, when the Mission, now rich in paintings, tapestries, vestments, statues, and relics of its early history, will return to the earth from which it sprung and, like many of the earlier Missions, be as a memory to those who come after. SHALL THIS BE?"

was a series of events that changed from year to year: contests and games for children and adults, a colorful costume ball on the first night, and a major outdoor event in the afternoon or evening of the second day, as conditions warranted.

The rodeo was, of course, the traditional event, just as it was in the earliest festivals in the mid-1800s. Like the early ones, the San Juan Bautista rodeo was for local cowboys from the surrounding area. Later it became part of the national network of rodeos.

It is easy to place definite dollar values on cash grants, but this is not so of the thousands of hours of work done by local supporters.

A news story in March 1929 in the *San Juan Mission News* gave a good insight into the value of volunteers.

"Over $2,500 Paid Into The Old Mission Fund," was the headline to the report of the collection from three contributions that week totaling $33.50. Not headlined was the further report of donations of labor and building materials. Joe Thomas donated ten days of work to design and maintain the trees and gardens; Frank Avilla and Ambrose Nunes, four days each with a team to haul sand; E. P. Giaccomazz, hauling five loads of cement from the plant; Joe Botello and Son, two days with team hauling sand; Frank Vincent, hauling fifty sacks of cement from the plant; George Neuther, hauling steel rods from San Jose; two loads of cement from the plant and one load of sand from San Juan Canyon. The Old Mission Portland Cement Company gave 650 sacks of cement and seventy-five yards of gravel. Granite Rock Company donated fifty tons of crushed granite rock. Frank Hudner donated iron and the labor in preparing it.

Such was the townspeople's enthusiastic support of the restoration of the mission in 1929. Little wonder that another headline on the same page read, "Complete Restoration of Old Mission a Possibility." The news story also outlined the plans of Tony Taix to organize an appeal to San Francisco friends.

It also revealed that the current restoration plans campaign was started "a month or six weeks ago when Steve Lavagnino took hold of the proposition with the aid of a committee ... " Local feeling was that "there has been since the disaster of 1906 a lot of talk but little action." This was an overstatement but it undoubtedly helped spark the current campaign to complete making the church safe for regular use.

That year the community directed its enthusiasm in a new direction. For the 132nd anniversary celebration of the founding of the mission, committees were formed to present a pageant the day before the anniversary, June 23, 1929.

Chatting between scenes of a mission pageant are, left to right, Louise Kurtyak, Irene Piccetti Barcala, an unidentified woman, and John Baumgartner, standing beside his horse.

A scene from a pageant and a small part of the audience at the 1930 pageant. All the pageants were presented on the Mission Plaza.

The first meeting of the planning committee was on May 24. Cement plant superintendent Frank F. Parker was named general chairman. For this special event the committee received support from Hollister and the smaller towns in the county. The planners rallied to the challenge to make this the largest celebration ever in "this old town," according to the *Mission News*.

Mayor Abbe headed plans for an information booth to supply visitors with historical material on San Juan Bautista. He also found a supplier in San Francisco for the costumes that would be needed. A man would be down within a week to show samples.

Frank Vincent reported that he had arranged for a truckload of ice cream and soda water and they needed some old horse troughs in which to keep the soda water cold. They could return what was not sold. It was suggested that women might help sell it but it was decided that "this might slack up trade, so it was decided to use only men."

George Abbe was chairman of the parade committee and had many details to clear up. The parade would start at the west end of Fourth Street, turn over to Third Street (remember that was High-

way 101 then), and go on to the middle of town before going to Second Street, where it would disband near the barbecue area. Mr. Dreisbach of the barbecue pit committee said he had forty-four men but needed six or seven reserves.

Steve Lavagnino reported he had 500 ribbons with an embossed metal bell and 1,000 plain ribbons with a bell printed on them. He bought them in San Francisco and was sure they could pay for them after the festival. The embossed ones would sell for fifty cents each.

The Castro building would serve as a museum. Musical program chairman William Kleckner reported he needed flute players. A week later he still needed one. The parade had an Indian float so they needed a Spanish float. Several women were appointed as ticket takers.

The pageant was written by Grace T. Mitchell of San Francisco and acted by the Santa Clara Passion Players under the direction of Edward Preston Murphy. Local men and women also acted in the pageant.

So it went in 1929, and so it has been through the years.

The Abbe Company was an enduring partnership of this era. Its store was at the southeast corner of Third and Polk. It was in the center of town as well as the center of most community events. Both partners, Frank and George, were destined to be mayors. The building has been enduring also. Built in 1860 to house Felipe Gardella's store, it was the only building in the block to survive the big fire of 1867. It has housed a bakery since 1938.

The people in the photo above are identified as: Albert Taix, Bud Hodges, George Abbe, Fred Kemp, (unknown), Annie Neelsey, Blondee Taix and Helen Neelsey.

(Top photo: SJB Historical Society public archives.)

Pageants were presented for several years without much change. The *Mission News* showed the degree of local participation by listing fifty-six participants one year. There were two local vocalists, two dancers of the fandango, and fifty-two members of the chorus, most of whom were women.

Attendance at the first pageant was estimated at eight thousand. The following years, in spite of the Great Depression, an almost full house was reported in the news for both afternoon and evening performances.

In 1934, citizens of San Juan Bautista took part in the Commemoration of Serra Year with an outstanding pageant. The commemorative year was officially proclaimed by the state legislature in memory of the 150th anniversary of the great founder's death. Five other old missions had similar presentations, all independent of each other. The one at Santa Clara Mission had a cast of 250 participants, according to the Reverend A. P. Spearman, S.J., in *The Call Board*, March 1935.

Special attractions in the late 1930s included horse shows and polo games. Pageants continued

A full program of all rodeo contests brought cowboys from all over the country to win points toward national titles.

not completed. A community committee was formed to study the problem, and by 1947 it came up with a winning formula for the mission fund and the town.

Arrangements were made with the national network of champion rodeos, the Professional Cowboys Association of America, for an annual date near June 24 for a rodeo in San Juan Bautista.

Improvements were made on the rodeo grounds at the bottom of the escarpment near the old mission church where the mission's pear orchard had once prospered. Grandstands on the face of the cliff were improved, and enlarged as necessary, over the next thirty-six years.

Each year there was an awakening of the community to welcome eight-to-nine thousand spec-

until 1941, but World War II prompted the cancellation of all community celebrations for the general public. The American Legion organized some town picnics with speakers and games on the Fourth of July.

Governors, lieutenant governors and other state officers were eager to speak before large audiences such as the festival audiences. That was, of course, before television when politicians were eager to meet constituents on a face to face basis. For local politicians it was an annual "must" on their calendar.

A reevaluation after World War II clearly showed that the task of restoring the mission was

Intermissions included a variety of events, such as this Benny Banion Stage Coach from Las Vegas in 1976.

tators to the rodeo. This usually meant crowds of up to twenty-five thousand over a weekend, in town for the parades, barbecues, balls, horse shows, and independent picnics.

The rodeo came at an opportune time for the mission restoration fund. In 1950 the Hearst Fund pledged a $25,000 contribution if that amount were raised by local contributions. The rodeo funds were not quite enough to match it immediately, but the town's commitment was accepted as adequate by the Hearst Fund. As a result, 1950 is generally cited as the year the restoration of the mission was completed.

It was also an opportune time for finding a corps of volunteers to take a major responsibility on the rodeo committee. The men and women

After the 1983 rodeo was over, the deserted grandstands remained as a reminder of thirty-six past fiestas.

Above the rodeo grandstands a plaque was placed calling attention to the small portion of the El Camino Real at the foot of the escarpment. The plaque tells some of its history. The Salinas Boy Scout Troop 233 earned a special history award for placement of the plaque.

coming home from service in the war had organized Veterans of Foreign Wars, Post No. 6359.

With the completion of their post headquarters, they wanted to make their presence felt in the community. The rodeo appealed to them, and a group of their members volunteered to take over a major job in the overall committee. In the second year of the rodeo, the V.F.W. group took charge of the supervision of the concessionaires and continued for thirty-four years.

Leonard Caetano had that job for the first rodeo. He turned to other tasks on the volunteer committee and in a short time was chairman, a post he filled for more than twenty-five years. At the same time he worked as assistant manager and then manager of the cement plant, until 1974. If he had any spare time, there was always a task or two for him at the city hall. For sixteen years, from 1962 to 1978, Caetano was mayor of San Juan Bautista, a record tenure for the office.

The rodeos continued until 1983 and contributed $750,000 to the mission restoration fund.

Because they were endorsed by the Professional Cowboys Association, the rodeos drew the best riders in the country, seeking points for the national championship titles in their events. Publicity went throughout northern California as well as to cowboys all over the nation. There was no cost to the town or the local merchants for this promotion which brought thousands of people to San Juan Bautista once a year.

While all this was happening, there were many other events in the town.

SAN JUAN GETS A RAILROAD

A major business opportunity for San Juan Bautista in the first decade of the twentieth century came in a double package. In 1906 a man, a stranger, arrived in San Juan and began asking many questions, checking nearby hills and waterways and then talking to businessmen. He left, still unknown, but was followed by others planning great things for the town.

First, they planned to bring in a railroad from the Southern Pacific Coast Line at Chittenden, six miles west of town.

Second, the railroad would make it feasible for a cement manufacturing plant to locate in the San Juan Canyon area. The town envisioned a payroll of two hundred to three hundred men.

The railroad was incorporated first as the San Juan Pacific Railway on May 4, 1907. As far back as 1880 there had been talk of a railroad from the Monterey Bay area to the San Joaquin Valley. It was developed to the point in 1881 that a survey was made over Mammoth Pass east of Fresno for a new transcontinental line in competition with the Southern Pacific. San Juan had good reason to be optimistic that the San Juan Pacific might be extended to Monterey and the San Joaquin Valley.

The route of the California Central Railroad, the operating name given this local unit, was: The railroad crossed the Pajaro River at Chittenden, followed the river eastward for two and a half miles; took a more southern direction for four miles; turned south to come up from the valley about a half a mile east of town; and ended at the factory site on the west side of San Juan Canyon.

A depot was built near the town, east of the junction of Third Street and the Alameda. The route to the cement plant went just about through the middle of the present site of the San Juan School.

Just three months after the first incorporation a second corporation, named San Juan Southern Railway Company, was organized to provide a six-mile railroad to Hollister. What lavish dreams that must have inspired. But nothing happened.

The sponsor of the railroad also incorporated the San Juan Portland Cement Company. They busied themselves buying all the machinery needed in the plant while the railroad was completed.

By September the California Central was ready and began bringing in tons of plant equipment.

Outgoing trains had to depend on the shipments from farmers. The first shipment was two carloads of barley.

In October the Southern Pacific announced that three passenger trains a day would stop at Chittenden for passengers to transfer to the California Central. A combination baggage-passenger car was supplied.

The appointment of Mark Regan as conductor, baggage manager, and express manager prompted Dorothy Flint to write, "The familiar presence of Mark Regan as ticket agent and conductor meant too, that the train trip to Chittenden Junction retained much of the flavor associated with the former stage ride between San Juan and Sargent's Station."

Another month brought a great change. The cement company had run out of money, and construction stopped. All the material was there, but the railroad lost its one big customer.

The railroad had to depend on agricultural freight and passenger service. The summer and fall shipments of hay, fruit from the Anderson Packing Company, and sugar beets gave the railroad some income.

In May 1908 passenger service was canceled, and Mark Regan went back to his stagecoach. Regan got

First Railroad to San Juan. Engine No. 208 of the San Juan Pacific and three cars of happy townspeople arrived in San Juan on August 31, 1907.

even with the railroad by telling everyone it was okay, because his stage was faster than the train.

The railroad may have been a factor in 1910 when another new industry came to the valley. It brought in twenty carloads of material for the C. C. Morse Seed Company. Mr. Morse had purchased 1,000 acres halfway between San Juan and Hollister, and for years people had a mass of color to admire as they passed the acres of flowers being grown for commercial seed. In 1930 a private partnership was formed by Morse and Dexter M. Ferry, and Ferry-Morse Seed Company was formed.

San Juan's first depot was built east of where Third Street turns into the Alameda.

San Juan Valley Echo.

VOL. IX.   SAN JUAN SAN BENITO COUNTY, CAL., SATURDAY, AUGUST 24, 1907.   NO. 45

Railroad Notes.

At a meeting held at the Plaza hotel Wednesday, with L. F. Rankin, A. Taix, Sr. and G. S. Tremaine, all the right-of-way was arranged for satisfactorily. This comples the right of way between Chittenden and the cement plant.

Mr W. C. Look, locating engineer for the San Joaquin Valley Western Railroad, gave a banquet at Hollister on the evening of the 22d instant. to the may r and prominent citizens of Hollister. Watsonville and other points. It was in the nature of a celebration of the commencement of actual work on the railroad.

Engineer Look says that the temporary connection of the San Juan Pacific with the Southern Pacific is for the purpose of getting machinery through to the cement works, and as soon as he has completed the survey of the San Joaquin Valley Western to Fresno he will return and run a line under the Southern Pacific at Chittenden, at a grade lower than the present one to bring connections between the new lines just named and the Ocean Shore and Eastern from Chittenden to Santa Cruz, where the Ocean Shore line to San Francisco will complete the through line from Fresno to the metropolis.

Dr. Kocher made a flying visit to San Jose Monday, transacting important business.

D. Mc Phail and J. H. Lynn of Hollister transacted business in this city

The Same Old Question.

What's the matter with yo 'phone?' is a question that is propounded to us every day. and "Shake up your 'phone, I can't hear a word you say." is what we hear every time we are called. We have examined the "insides" of the machine and came to the conclusion, from our diagnosis, that it needed a set of new batteries, and so informed "Central", but we haven't seen the new batteries yet. If every ones 'phone batteries are in the shape our office 'phone's are. we don't wonder at people kicking. for they have a kick coming. Come now, Mr. Pacific States Telephone and Telegraph Company, and see what you can do for us, for we might miss some important news, all because of the condition of our telephone.

The many friends of Miss Rosalie Taix will be pleased to learn that she graduaten from the San Jose Business College last Friday with high honors. She will return home next week.

Elmer and Ralph Dunham, of Salinas, were over Sunday.

Dan Martin will leave Monday for Portland, Oregon, where he will have charge a large foundry at that place.

Mr. and Mrs. A. S. Moore visited at the home of Mr. and Mrs. Will Flint in Fairview last Sunday.

The Misses May Regan and Maud Goodwin visited in Hollister Wednesday.

Cement News

The work of grading and excavating for the large kiln building has been practically completed. The foundations for the stock house are finished and the frame is being erected.

Prospecting on the Barbee, Flint and Underwood quarries is being rushed and some fine looking rock is being brought ont.

All the concrete used in the construction work will be set by the Ransome Construction Company.

The narrow gauge locomotive to be used on the quarry road is at Miller's siding and will be brought up as soon as needed.

Mrs. M. Antonelli and daughter were over from Santa Cruz the first of the week, superintending the work on their hotel on the Alameda.

Mr. and Mrs. Robert Larios were down from San Francisco this week visiting their cousin Miss M. Salas.

N. F. Gobar is soon to erect a modern cottage on his lot on First street. The contract for the lumber has allready been given to the new lumber yard here.

Carmel Martin, of Monterey, is transacting business in town.

Frank Abbe is attending to business in San Jose and the Bay cities.

The erection of the Antoinella

Local and Personal.

On account of the non-arrival of our usual bundle of papers subscribers will receive but six pages in place of ten pages.

Lem Townsend was over from Hollister yesterday.

The Abbe Co., have installed an up- to- date National Cash Register in their store.

Miss J. C. Dougherty returned to Lonetree Sunday, having spent the week's end with her mother near town.

J J. Burt, an attorney from San Francisco, was in town on business Saturday last.

W. F. Duncan and family are at home again, having broken camp at Chittenden.

Mrs. A Taix and children, Marie and Albert, are guests of relatives in the Bay cities

J. F. Cleveland, of the Echo office, visited with friends in Hollister Sunday.

M. J. Regan Jr. spent Saturday and Sunday with his parents here, combining business with pleasure.

Miss Rose Regan was down from an Francisco last week, visiting the

Misses Cynthia Bersinger and Viola Prescot have resumed their studies at the High School in Hollister

---

San Juan Valley Echo, August 24, 1907. The volume number indicates publication started in 1898. Good news coverage includes plans for a basket picnic in Taix's grove followed by a grand ball in Plaza Hall on the day the first railroad arrives. Ramona Heights would soon open with a $50,000 tourist hotel.

Cement news included: "The large kiln building has been practically completed. . . . Prospecting on the Barbee, Flint and Underwood quarries is being rushed. . . . The narrow gauge locomotive . . . is at Miller's siding and will be brought up as soon as needed." A survey of the San Joaquin Valley Western to Fresno was planned.

In 1969 it was sold to the Purex Corporation, and now on 110 acres they only do research and development of new varieties of vegetables.

The winters of 1909-10 and 1910-11 were wet years, and the railroad suffered from washouts, but then a light appeared at the end of the tunnel.

San Juan Portland Cement Company was sold to a new corporation, the Old Mission Cement Company, in January 1912. By May there was talk about various expansions of the railroad, but no action. San Juan Pacific ended up with its original 7.94 miles.

Construction of the plant had started in November 1912. All the delays, rumors, forlorn hopes, disappointments, etc. are not known, but a casual look at a few newspapers indicates that there were many dates and many promises not kept.

THE SAN JUAN STAR

Vol. I   SAN JUAN, SAN BENITO COUNTY, CALIFORNIA, AUGUST 31, 1907   No. 35

Rancher Meets Death Under Load of Hay

An unfortunate accident occurred near Tres Pinos last Friday in which Domingo Furtado met death and Domingo Roger had several ribs broken and was otherwise badly bruised.

The two men had started from the Azhe ranch with a load of hay and a four-horse team. Coming down a hill near Tres Pinos, the brake broke allowing the heavily loaded wagon to run on the horses which started the animals to going. The driver lost control of the horses and the wagon fell over. Furtado was caught beneath several tons of hay while Roger was more fortunate. Help was summoned and the hay was removed as soon as possible. Furtado was alive and conscious but died very soon thereafter.

John Etcheverry of Tres Pinos brought Roger to Hollister in his automobile where he was placed under the care of a physician.

Dr. O'Bannon was hurriedly taken to the scene of the accident but it was too late as Furtado was beyond human aid. The remains were brought to Hollister for burial.

Domingo Furtado was a native of Azores and was aged twenty-seven years. He was known as an industrious young man and was highly respected by all who knew him. This was his first season at ranching for himself and had just harvested his first crop. He was a member of the I. D. E. S. society under whose auspices the funeral was conducted. He was an unmarried man but leaves two brothers to mourn his loss.

The funeral took place Sunday, August 25, 1907, and a large crowd attended.

[No. 1 band wagon] for hire cheap or will trade for hay or wood. Apply at this office.   tf

Grand Reception and Banquet Given the San Juan Pacific Officials

Officials of the San Juan Portland Cement Company Also Honored--A Great Event.

The Old Mission Town has again placed a big mark on the right side of the ledger. The new era of progress for San Juan and the valley was sealed with the acceptance of the railroad officials of the San Juan Pacific railroad from the contractors. For years the old town has been endeavoring to get a railroad and yesterday her hopes were realized.

Yesterday a representative crowd of business men journeyed from the San Juan end of the road to Chittenden, where they met the officials of the railroad and cement company and after a general introduction the party returned by rail to Taix's Grove. Just as the train pulled in the band struck up a welcoming tune, and amidst the shrieking of whistles, the roar of anvils, the clanging of bells and the cheering of the crowd; the officials landed in San Juan.

After the tumult had subsided, with a few well chosen words Attorney Geo. Moore welcomed the gentlemen to our town. We assured them we appreciated the effort they had put forth to get a line here. We also assured them that both the people of San Juan and the valley would give the company after its completion the heartiest support from our people. Mr. Brown, President of the Cement Company, in behalf of the officials, thanked Mr. Moore for his kind words. He assured the people the company appreciated the public spirit displayed and he sincerely hoped the relations would always be the same.

The officials were then driven to the Plaza hotel and after a short rest were ushered into the banquet hall, where plates were set for sixty guests. The menu no doubt was the most elaborate the hostelry ever spread, and well might it be, as probably never before in the history of the hotel had there been such a representative body of men gathered around the table on this occasion.

Mr. S. R. Canfield acted as toastmaster and the following toasts were responded to:

San Juan Portland Cement Co. and the San Juan Pacific Railroad, Mr. Frank L. Brown.

Electrical Engineering for California, Mr. Beach

This issue of the *San Juan Star*, Vol. 1, No. 35, of August 31, 1907, indicated this was its first year of publication, but records in City Hall show that A. B. Shaw and the *Star* were paid for carrying legal advertising and for office supplies in June 1904. There is no obvious answer to this puzzle from the facts at hand.

Published the day after arrival of the first railroad in San Juan, the *Star* can tell us about the celebration for this long awaited day by townspeople. It reported, " . . . a representative crowd of business men journeyed . . . to Chittenden where they met the officials of the railroad and cement company . . . and returned by rail to Taix's Grove."

The "new era of progress for San Juan" was the theme of the entire article. The band greeted them at the park and the program went on. There was a banquet with many speakers, and the ball lasted" into the wee hours of the morning."

Attorney G. Moore spoke on "awakening of San Juan from her long sleep."

San Juan Valley Echo.
and the SAN JUAN STAR

VOL. XXXIX   SAN JUAN, SAN BENITO COUNTY, CAL., SATURDAY, MAY 28, 1910   NO. 23

The *San Juan Valley Echo and the San Juan Star*, May 28, 1910, shows a consolidation had become necessary. The following year the *Valley Echo* discontinued publication. No major community news appears on the front page, the only page available. It does reveal within four months after organizing, the Native Daughters of the Golden West was planning "the erection of a Mission Bell, June 24." Plans were also underway for "a grand ball and a supper in the old Mission banquet hall."

One was outside of San Juan. The 1915 State Mining Journal carried a major article about the new plant at San Juan Bautista which started production in 1914. So they were one year early? No. So they were two years early? Well, no, but there is one source that said production started in 1916. But let us go on to 1918 where news articles are more specific.

A short report in the *San Juan Mission News* of May 6, 1918, read, "The Cement Plant Has Started Up." Well, yes, they had started getting some of the ingredients together. "The plant is practically started, and the doubting Thomases need have no fear but that it will continue to operate."

Three weeks later, on May 25, the headline was, "Finished Product Is Turned Out Of Cement Plant!" "Of course," the article said, "the first operation of new machinery causes some little trouble . . . the demand for the cement is great, and the future is rosy with two carloads of cement being shipped daily."

Finally, three months later, on August 21, 1918, the Hunt Engineering Company declared the plant completely installed and turned it over to the Old Mission Portland Cement Company to operate.

When construction started in 1912 completion was scheduled for 1914. And the first promise of a cement plant had been made in 1907, eleven years earlier than the official completion of construction in 1918.

The eleven years had many false promises, new plans, rumors, and disappointments. The above is probably typical of all that the town went through.

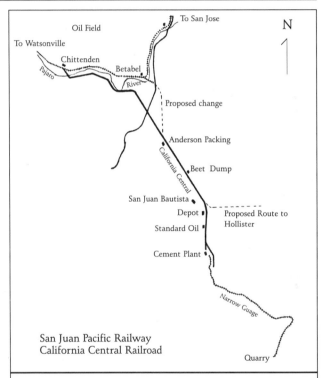

Map of the 7.94-mile connection between Chittenden and San Juan and the early rail lines in the cement plant.

It is unfortunate, but understandable, that they failed to build homes for the workers. The *Mission News* felt otherwise and castigated the town in mid-1918 because "today there is not a single modern house in town that can be rented."

Records show there were a few homes built after the war, but not enough. Five bungalows were built in 1915 and three years later construction began on eight more modern bungalows. O. F. Lindburgh of Oakland was in charge of construction, on Polk Street near Fourth Street, for the

Employees of the Old Mission Portland Cement Company pose for a company portrait circa 1915. The original cement company had scheduled 664 carloads of machinery and materials. All had arrived by November 1907 and remained for these buidlings, so far as is known.

Ramona Heights Land Company. Lindburgh was enthusiastic about the potential growth of San Juan and announced that he was going to make this his home. Many more homes were built around Ramona Heights in the 1920s. The word Heights, however, was somewhat of a misnomer. Old-timers remembered some of the area best as having several large mud puddles.

After three, or four, or five, or more delays in the building of the cement plant, it is likely that contractors or investors wouldn't build new homes on the basis of yet another promise.

It is possible their lack of confidence in the future did not end when construction was completed. Cement plants, like many components of the building industry, operated in cycles. A long period of reduced orders would be cause for a temporary shutdown. The operation of a cement plant is a complex procedure requiring close chemical controls at every step, and there were over eighty separate operations before good cement was made. A skeleton crew cannot produce a satisfactory product in a cement plant, so periodic total layoffs are not unusual.

Production went well, as reflected in a news article January 3, 1920, which told of a record shipment of sixteen carloads in one day. The entire shipment was for export to foreign ports including South America and the Hawaiian Islands.

In the mid-1920s, Old Mission Portland Cement Company was paying a dividend of forty cents per year on common stock selling at two dollars per share, and preferred stockholders were also being paid regularly.

There appeared no need in 1927 for Old Mission to sell, consolidate or merge (all terms were used by one announcement) with Pacific Portland Cement Company. This was announced in February 1927 and was considered a case of a larger firm wanting to become larger.

The name of Old Mission was still used in June 1928 when the company announced that construction had started on a three and a half mile extension of the narrow gauge railroad to a new quarry in the upper canyon. At the same time superintendent Frank Parker announced mill work would be renewed immediately and would continue. The following month a more detailed report of production plans was issued in the name of Pacific Portland Cement Company.

The name meant little when in 1929 the plant became an early casualty of the Great Depression.

The San Juan Pacific Railroad was given permission in 1931 to suspend service. This was renewed year by year, and in 1933 they started liquidation of assets, which was not completed until 1943. This was done in the name of Pacific Portland Cement Company.

Except for rails imbedded in pavement at the entrance to San Juan Canyon there is little left to show of the old railroad to Chittenden.

In 1941 the Pacific Portland plant reopened to supply wartime needs. Trucks replaced both railroads. The limestone was brought from a quarry seven miles south of the plant on a private usage road in trucks that carried from thirty to thirty-one tons per trip.

The Ideal Cement Company was just south of town at the entrance to San Juan Canyon. This picture could be of any workday from 1955 to 1972.

The plant had a good record during the war, supplying both domestic and overseas needs of the armed forces. It was obliged to close down in 1945 when government buying ended and postwar building had not yet started.

Pent-up demands for building, roads and repairs were substantial, and in 1947 the plant reopened. The Pacific Portland Cement Company sold the plant to Ideal Cement Company of Denver, Colorado, in 1955.

The sale did not interrupt work; in fact there was only one plant closing between 1947 and 1972. Ideal maintained a full crew of 140 to 160 during this period.

In the late 1960s Ideal began plans to increase output with not only a new, more modern plant, but also a new plan to transport the stone from the quarry to the plant. The plan would eliminate all dust enroute by mixing the rocks with water to wash it all down to the plant.

Ideal Cement budgeted $60,000,000 for the modernization program. State and local requirements forced Ideal to consider revising its budget. An increase to $100,000,000 appeared to be necessary, but such a cost could not be justified by possible income in the foreseeable future. In 1972 the plant was closed.

After more than twenty years, it is best to leave the closing of Ideal Cement with this dollars-and-cents explanation, with just a word of thanks to the three companies for the free cement, rock, and many favors given to the town, the mission, and many other worthwhile activities.

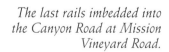

The last rails imbedded into the Canyon Road at Mission Vineyard Road.

A group of local historians decided in 1993 that the railroad should not be forgotten. Working with the Monterey Viejo Chapter 1846 of E Clampus Vitus, a statewide organization that advocates historical markers, the group arranged for a detailed monument memorializing the railroad's role in local history.

THE SAN JUAN PACIFIC RAILWAY WAS
INCORPORATED MAY 4, 1907, BECOMING THE
CALIFORNIA CENTRAL RAILROAD IN 1912.
SOME OF THE LOCALS REFERRED TO IT AS THE
SAN JUAN TERRIFIC. BUILT TO HAUL THE
EXPECTED LARGE QUANTITIES OF PORTLAND
CEMENT FROM THE OLD MISSION CEMENT COMPANY
PLANT NEARBY, THE MAINLINE EXTENDED 7.94
MILES FROM CHITTENDEN TO SAN JUAN JUNCTION.
CEASING RAILROAD OPERATIONS IN 1930, THE TRACK
WAS RIPPED UP AFTER THE LAST LOCOMOTIVE,
OCEAN SHORE NO. 5 WAS STEAMED UP AND SHIPPED
TO NEVADA IN 1937. A NARROW GAUGE 'ROAD' REACHED
THE LIMESTONE QUARRY UP THE SAN JUAN CANYON.

DEDICATED SATURDAY MORNING AUGUST 14, 1993
MONTEREY VIEJO CHAPTER 1846
E CLAMPUS VITUS

It was dedicated on August 14, 1993, "with all the ceremonial pomp fit for a presidential inauguration," one newspaper said. "With parade, musical entertainment, dedication and barbecue, the group eternalized that which time has nearly erased." The plaque was designed by Valerie Egland.

In the photo above, local historians and some of the speakers at the dedication bracket the monument.

From left, Jack Baxter and Albert D. Snyder, who spoke of their railroad days; Louise Perry, ninety-three-year-old San Juan native; Leonard Caetano, former cement plant manager and mayor; and Richard A. Gularte, realtor and early president of the San Juan Bautista Historical Society.

AND THE TOWN MOVED ON

The town moved out of the very eventful first decade of the twentieth century in high spirits, but it is apparent that enthusiasm ebbed as they struggled to support their railroad with local freight while the cement factory rusted in San Juan Canyon. By 1912 the town had lost its two newspapers and it was 1914 before another publisher arrived to launch publication of the *San Juan Mission News*.

With all available copies of the *Mission News* on microfilm in the city library, all the day-to-day changes of the town's good or bad fortunes are reported. That would be tedious reading, but major events or trends can be ferreted out or supported by these "first rough drafts of history," as newspapers are sometimes called. Historians and the public are indebted to the San Juan Bautista Historical Society and Library Auxiliary for underwriting the cost of microfilm equipment so library patrons can review the issues of the *San Juan Mission News*.

Charles Morse, with his commercial seed farm, was in the vanguard of new crops on the lands around San Juan Bautista. His seed business prospered over the years, and many other seed growers have developed nearby acreage.

Strawberry farms were popular with Japanese farmers. A news article in 1916 said, "Strawberries from California mean of course strawberries from the San Juan valley where the finest berries in the state and possibly in the entire world are grown." It also said the local berries sold at a premium in San Francisco.

The dollar value of the berries was reported as excellent for both the Japanese farmers and the land owners. At that time, foreign-born Japanese were not allowed to own land under California law.

The Japanese farmers grew other crops and were a major part of the agriculture community through the years until Pearl Harbor. Their removal from the area to detention camps in the interior disrupted their lives, and many did not return to the valley.

An unusual crop being grown by W. S. Hayden since 1908 was featured in the *Free-Lance* in 1916. It was spineless cactus. He had received orders from Cuba, Mexico and Ecuador as well as many ranches in the United States. Only one other grower was identified, but there must have been others as Hayden's plants were rated as among the "finest cactus in the county." He had twenty varieties; one was named "San Juan." The cactus were grown for cattle feed, and because the slabs contained a large amount of water, they were most in demand in dry areas.

Hayden and his family moved to San Juan in 1894 when he bought the Plaza Hotel from Angelo Zanetta. Hayden operated it until 1905 when he sold it to Antoine Taix, Jr. He owned several business buildings in Hollister, but his home was on his two-and-one-half-acre cactus ranch near San Juan.

World War I

After the United States entered the war in Europe in 1917, both men and women from San Juan enlisted in the armed services or joined in support activities on the home front.

In May of 1918 San Juan received an honor flag bearing three stripes and two stars. The town had not only exceeded its quota of money for the third Liberty Loan, it had subscribed to more than three times its quota.

"The flag would be hung across Third Street so that all who pass may be informed that this is not a city of slackers, but patriots who believe in doing more than is expected of the people," said the *Mission News* on its front page.

This was the dominant spirit. When a drive was conducted for money, the paper published a list of donors and the amount each gave.

Women helped in many drives, but they also had their own organized committees under councils of national and state defense. The San Benito County committees had numerous subcommittees.

One of the first projects in 1917 was a flea market. It was repeated in 1918. The San Benito County committee had a Thrift Stamp Drive run by a militant company of young women.

The women made a request of the U.S. Army and Navy. In a resolution they wrote, "Whereas, in the army and navy of our country the nurses are given no recognition and only by courtesy are they of higher rank than scrub women . . . " Their request for recognition of the nurses was undoubtedly expressed elsewhere and contributed to improved conditions.

Agricultural production was important and the San Juan Valley did its best despite the loss of many patriotic young men who went into the service. As might be expected, women pitched in when fruits and other crops had to be harvested during the shortage of manpower. They also solicited books to be sent to troops in nearby camps.

Local news and national news were filled with stories about the war effort.

The First National Bank of San Juan

San Juan Bautista progressed during the war years and entered the postwar era with confidence for a prosperous future.

The most impressive event of the postwar era in San Juan was undoubtedly the opening of the First National Bank of San Juan in 1919. Before it opened all banking had to be done in adjoining towns or larger cities such as San Francisco, Oakland or San Jose.

The First National Bank was an independent operation but was sponsored by the Bank of Italy, which later became the Bank of America. Local stockholders bought nearly half the initial stock offering, buying from one to ten shares each.

The first announcement of plans for a bank was in early February. On March 1, 1919 the opening date of March 10 was announced.

Depositors arrived early on opening day, and the honor of being the first depositor fell to six-year-old Joe Cravea, Jr., son of local shoe store owners Mr. and Mrs. Joe Cravea, Sr. While young Joe's coins were being counted, another clerk completed the first deposit for Frank B. Abbe, who had only checks to deposit.

The officers were Thomas B. Hawkins, president and an organizer of the Bank of Hollister in 1873; Steve Lavagnino, vice president and local businessman; and R. H. Pearce, cashier and former Bank of Italy employee in San Jose. Directors were Frank B. Abbe, businessman; W. S. Hayden, businessman; Antoine Taix, investor; George Wapple, Hollister druggist; and W. E. Blauer, manager of the San Jose branch of the Bank of Italy.

The bank leased a building which was referred to as the east wing of the Tony Taix Building, on Third Street near Mariposa. The Bank of America was later built on the land adjacent to the First National Bank.

"Sewer Bonds Carry By 10 to 1 Majority" read a headline in the *Mission News* of April 3, 1920. The voters were obviously anxious for action. For over a year the newspaper had been agitating for action on this important public service.

Two weeks later the annual municipal election was "very quiet," possibly because the most important issue had been settled—they thought.

Seven months later city engineers presented plans for the entire project. The trustees accepted the plans and started "looking about with a view of disposing the bonds to the best advantage."

Another seven months and the bonds were sold to the State Board of Control. The money was placed in the vault of the San Juan First National Bank. Before the money was needed, the bank borrowed some of it. That was in May 1921.

Four months more and the sewer question was still in the talking stage. In fact, the trustees called a breakfast meeting "a talkfest." They may have talked, but the town engineer failed to show up with needed details. That was September 16, 1921, sixteen months after the 10 to 1 vote.

By the next July—two years and three months after the 10 to 1 vote—a newspaper headline read, "Town Trustees Hire Legal Help To Guide Them For Sewer Lines." It seems they were having trouble with some property owners who did not want to sign right-of-ways for some sewer lines across their prop-

The First National Bank was located in the one-story building left of the Taix Building. The successor, the Bank of America, is now to the left and behind this building.

The interior of the Bank of Italy at 10:45 the morning of the twenty-first of some month in 1920. All this from the clock on the wall. Just think of all the adjustments if the clock is not wound someday. David White stands at extreme left.

the previous month. This ordinance raised business taxes 100 to 300 percent, increasing local taxes to 500 percent more than taxes in nearby towns.

One trustee's reply was, "If you can't pay this unheard of extortionate tax, better get out of business." Three others agreed, and nothing immediate came of the protest.

However, by early December recall petitions had been filed against these four trustees. Other complaints included the charge that a new marshal had been hired for one hundred and forty dollars per month although an existing ordinance contained a limit of sixty dollars per month and that the town attorney, who was paid a monthly salary, was improperly paid for ordinances the trustees had him draw. Added to these were objections to the "insolent, contemptuously and insulting remarks and demeanor of the four trustees." An election was set for February 22, 1922.

All four trustees were recalled by a margin of about 10 to 7 votes in each case. Elected were Frank B. Abbe, who was named mayor, a post he held for ten years until his death; Frank M. Vincent; Fred J. Beck; and S. Lavagnino.

The new trustees were all successful businessmen and guided the town well. At the first meeting they rehired CC Zanetta as constable. He had continued some of his duties in his dual role as a deputy sheriff during the three months he had been replaced.

erty. "Members of the board are extremely anxious to get to work on the sewers as soon as possible." That was mid-July 1922.

They did get action, and soon Third Street had pipelines, and then the Alameda, and so on around town.

However, the trustees were doing other things which, by October, were giving them big trouble. On October 10, a delegation appeared before the board to protest Ordinance 74A, which had been passed

Chautauqua Comes to Town

The Chautauqua came to San Juan Bautista on June 1, 1920.

The Chautauqua was a famous name then as for forty-six years it had been presenting programs across the nation. The name is that of a town in upstate New York where it originated. Its goal was to bring a series of programs for entertainment, education and inspiration of a caliber not otherwise available to smaller towns. Audience discussion was encouraged.

A coordinator had arrived in early March to determine if the town wanted a Chautauqua season. It would only come if the public subscribed for 200 season tickets. For each two-and-a-half-dollar pledge they offered seven performances, three in the afternoon and four in the evening.

The *Mission News* supported the Chautauqua and told the public, "None but high class artists are employed, and a change in the personnel every day. The members who furnish the entertainment on the first day leave the next morning, and an entirely new set of ten artists arrive and furnish the entertainment for the next day. So on throughout the four days. No artist appears oftener than the one day's performance. When we say artists, we mean real artists, men and women who stand high in the profession."

Among the performers were a noted lecturer, a poet/humorist, a Gypsy Girls quartet, and musicians presenting excerpts from Gilbert and Sullivan.

The price today seems reasonable, but these were the days of nickel and dime movies. The town did reach its goal of 200 pledges, and based on the record of the Chautauqua, it is probable that they enjoyed "the high class programs" promised in the newspaper.

By 1920, the era of the Chautauqua was about over. It was being replaced by the radio, movies and phonographs. Faster and easier transportation to urban areas allowed everyone to enjoy a variety of art, education and entertainment.

San Juan Bautista did have its own movie house in 1920. The Star Theater had opened three years earlier and maintained a flexible schedule of production probably depending on the popularity of the "high class" movies it offered.

By 1920 residents of San Juan Bautista were ready for a well-known town planning expert to tell

San Juan boosters made annual caravans in the mid-twenties to the Monterey-Carmel area to publicize local fiestas and other attractions. This may be a caravan leaving on the Coast Highway. Time was allowed for fishing in the river at Carmel.

them of their future possibilities. The man was Charles M. Goethe of Sacramento, a member of the California City Planning Commission.

"He was extremely enthusiastic over the latent opportunities of San Juan . . . with a little effort . . . made the most attractive summer and winter resort . . . universal style of Spanish architecture for homes and business buildings . . . thousands of tourists who are on search for such a place," and a few more suggestions and admonitions.

The town had already adopted some of the entertainment, cultural and promotional programs suggested by the visitor from Sacramento.

"Donations to Mission Fund Grow." This headline in the *Mission News* of March 1, 1923, is typical of the continued community support given to the repair of the mission.

Contributors are listed line by line with the amount donated by each. Total for the week was $555.60. Added to the amounts of the previous weeks, there was a grand total of $2,114.00.

More solicitations followed, and a report was given on the progress of plans for the June fiesta.

Mayor Frank B. Abbe had two news items for the *Mission News* on February 14, 1928. One was that all the sidewalks had been finished on Third Street and many were being laid on the Alameda.

Even better news was that the state was going to widen Third Street. In conversation with the state highway engineer, the mayor learned that "five feet will be added to the present highway." The highway, then named the Coast Highway and now Highway 101, was routed over the main streets of town. The additional paving would eliminate most of the mud and dust. Work would begin almost immediately and be of great benefit to travelers as well as the town.

Optimism dimmed shortly after when state surveyors began work on a realignment of the Coast Highway. Known as the Prunedale Cutoff, the new route would almost certainly remove the north-south traffic from San Juan.

By March 1930 the California Highway Commission decided to eliminate the San Juan grade as a part of the Coast Highway. (It was later returned to the system.) In its place would be a new highway three miles west of San Juan.

The cutoff might not have been so bad if provision had been made for a good state road for the three miles between the new highway and San Juan. The "Prunedale Cutoff," a dirty name to most people in San Benito County, was officially opened to traffic on July 20, 1932. The dedication drew about two hundred people, many of them officials from Monterey and Santa Cruz counties and from Gilroy, but none from San Benito County.

The historic bar of the Plaza Hotel as it was in 1935. The picture is a reminder that Prohibition had recently ended. Perennial constable CC Zanetta is far right, and next to him is a judge from San Francisco enjoying a day in the country.

Three years later District Engineer L. H. Gibson wrote in a state publication about the three-mile strip: "The motorist wishing to visit the picturesque mission town of San Juan Bautista was compelled to travel over the old and dangerous San Juan Grade, or over an old winding graveled county road, known as the Rocks Road because of its origin at the Pinecate Rocks through which the new Prunedale Cutoff runs."

By the following year, 1933, public-spirited citizens were able to get the problem before the legislature, and it made Rock Road a part of the state highway system. It was temporarily improved with an oil and screening seal.

By 1935 a portion of Rock Road near San Juan was rerouted and properly paved, and minimal road signs were provided. The 2.6 miles of road not only provided an easy way to reach San Juan from the Coast Highway but also gave all of San Benito County and the interior valleys a new route to the coast counties.

For three years the community worked for an impressive entrance where the 2.6-mile lateral turns from the Prunedale. On July 24, 1938, the *Mission News* reported that adobe bricks were being made across from the ballpark for "an elaborate affair being comprised of large adobe walls on both sides of the huge 'Y' shaped entrance." This was one of the most attrative signs but revision of the intersection obstructed the view so it was removed.

World War II

The war from 1941 to 1945 brought changes in San Juan Bautista as in all towns. Some of the major ones have been mentioned elsewhere. Greater production, morale, financing, communications, conservation, and many other actions are temporary and not true historic changes.

Local women, older men, students and others who could spare the time were often called upon to go out for light work, packing or

The construction on this marker, begun in 1934, was completed circa 1950 at highways 101 and 156 with the help of local volunteers.

harvesting. A pear ranch had a huge crop to pick in August of 1943 and called for thirty pickers from town to supplement forty Mexican nationals from a mobile labor camp in Hollister. The response reportedly was good.

Good response to all wartime appeals was not unusual in San Juan Bautista.

MEMORIES OF EARLY YEARS
Notes from Lodge Records

For the centennial celebration of Texas Lodge No. 46, F. & A. Masons, some unnamed members selected vignettes of the lodge's history. Primary source was the minutes of the lodge, and many items reflected an action or a state of conditions in San Juan.

The centennial observance was held in the Hall of Texas Lodge, Tuesday, November 11, 1953 which of course was and is the stately Masonic Building on Second Street. The lodge played an important role in the history of the town.

From the four pages of vignettes, only items that reflect conditions in the town and the use of their building are included in the following.

In the year 1853 a group of Texans decided to form a Masonic lodge in San Juan. They were part of a group of forty-two who had come from their native state shortly after the Mexican question in that area was settled.

The dispensation to form Texas Lodge was granted October 23, 1853. There was no record kept of early meetings, but after February 4, 1854, the minutes tell this story: By the end of 1854 the lodge had twenty members. By the end of 1867 it had 110 members.

No meeting place was mentioned until 1858 when the National Hotel was built at Second and San Jose streets, one block north of where the Masons later built their building. They met in a narrow hall, the third story of the hotel. "The bitter days of the Civil War era apparently had their repercussions in the lodge, for there is considerable mention of trials being held. One such trial for shooting a man resulted in exoneration for reasons of 'self defense.'"

In 1874, a very slack period seemed to set in. During the next twenty-five years, from 1874 to 1899, only twenty new members were admitted into the lodge.

Two entries in the 1880s told of the lodge's participation in St. John's Day observance by "procession, oration, basket picnic and dancing in Breen Grove." It was apparently an annual event such as a Fourth of July celebration.

In 1891 "the city council started using the downstairs space . . . for a monthly fee of one dollar. The Justice of the Peace also used one room for court sessions at a fee of fifty cents per case. The following year the San Juan Farmers Alliance asked that their rent be reduced to $2.50 and it was."

The United States Post Office rented space at four dollars per month in 1895. A milliner rented the "middle room" for two dollars per month in 1896.

1943 Red Cross War Fund Drive Started in County

County House-to-House Canvass Starts March 17

LOCAL SERVICE CLUB MEMBERS GIVE $100 TO DRIVE WEDNESDAY

New Rules for Overseas Mail

● New instructions pertaining mail for Army personnel over has just been released, according to

Local Men Leave For Army Exams Yesterday Morn

Gasoline Rations May Be Denied Truck Buyers

VOLUNTEERS NEEDED TO ASSIST WITH WAR RATION NO. TWO FEB. 22 TO 27

● Residents of this dist ister for R the

February 15.

There is not any penalty for ex cess ned goods to be

About Face!

Have you thought War Savings Stamps dignity—that W. S. S. were only for your chilc

Have you thought that Liberty Bonds were method of helping to finance the war?

No matter what your subscription to the Libe War Savings Stamps are also *for you!*

Friday, June 28th
National War Savings Day

An exact quota, according to population, has been set. It is $20 average for each American man, woman and child—this means the limit, $1000 each, for those who can, to average those who cannot.

The goal is $2,000,000,000 (Two Billion Dollars) to be obtained this year, 1918, which means to you···

About, Face!

Subscribe for your full quota of W. S. S.

W.S.S.   **National War Savings Committee**

County Exceeds War Bond Quota

● According to a report by Roy Petersen, chairman of the San B ito county war bond commmi the county again exceeded its Bond quota during January and February, going o the top by more than $42,000.

NDGW Purchase Another $100 War Bond

County House-to-House Canvass Starts March 17

LOCAL SERVICE CLUB MEMBERS GIVE $100 TO DRIVE WEDNESD

VOLUNTEERS NEEDE ASSIST WITH WAR R NO. TWO FEB. 22 T(

The following Mission News *story is only one example of the town's support during the war effort: "San Juan Bautista and surrounding area went over the top in the Third War Loan Drive Monday, when a total of $140,575 was turned in!*

"The quota for this city and the area was $135,000, and residents can well be proud of the fact that the sum was oversubscribed on Monday by $5,375.00."

BUILDINGS FROM THE PAST

There's quite a number of buildings, both commercial and residence, in San Juan Bautista that have beeen around for 100 years or more.

Many of them are on Third Street which has been the business center of the town for more than one hundred and fifty years.

For over half that time it was the main highway for all north-south traffic in western California. Most recently, the Coast Highway and then Highway 101 have been the most traveled routes. Before that there was El Camino Real, Old Stage Road, and San Juan Grade Road.

If you arrive in San Juan from Highway 101 or either western entrance, you will probably come to the end of Third Street. This sight will greet you. The large white building on the left was built in 1869 as a school building. The Odd Fellows Lodge bought it in 1907 and moved it to this location. The building on the right was built as the Bluebird Hotel in 1894 and later converted to apartments.

The above panorama is from the west end of Third Street. Below and on the next page is a photo parade of third-street buildings begining at the east end with one of the oldest buildings in town.

103 Third Street. *Casa Juan de Anza adobe residence was built in 1834. Almost 100 years later it became the first antique store in town*

107 Third Street. *The Casa Rosa, built in 1870 with a New England influence. A very popular restaurant featuring an early California menu has occupied it for many years.*

115 Third Street. *A one-story adobe built in 1850. It was believed to have been used as a bar. Theophile Vaché soon bought it to use as a marketing place for wines from his vineyards at Cienega.*

111 Third Street. *Behind Vaché's was a two-story adobe. It has been rebuilt many times. The most recent was a complete remodeling for an indoor-outdoor restaurant, El Jardin de San Juan, and offices. Next to it is a frame building, circa 1870.*

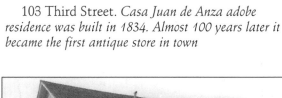

After the bakery, The Lavagnino family operated a general store on the lower floor for the next fifty years. Other commercial uses followed, including the Plaza Market downstairs and living quarters upstairs. Stephen Lavagnino and his wife are shown in front of their store early in the twentieth century.

203 Third Street. *Tuccoletta Hall, across from Vaché's, is a Monterey Colonial adobe of 1840. The hall upstairs accommodated orderly meetings, or lively, even wild dances through its many years, as well as the first movies shown in San Juan. Downstairs was first a tavern and then a bakery until the 1880s.*

300 and 302-4 Third Street. *The building on the right was built in 1856 by Jose Maria Castro. In 1865 Julius Brietbarth bought the building for a boot shop. For several years it has been the Mission Cafe. The building to the left dates from 1870. The Mission Shoe Renewal and Cravea Retail Clothing Store have been under continuous operation since 1906.*

The 300 block of Third Street *is dominated by the A. Taix Building. In 1867 a fire wiped out the entire block except a brick building, which was built in 1860. For many years it was the general merchandise store of Abbe and Co., and then a bakery. When the block was rebuilt, circa 1868-70, most of the buildings included some sandstone. All of the buildings other than the A. Taix Building, the early bank, and the Abbe building have been destroyed and replaced. This picture was taken in 1894.*

304A, 306, 308 Third Street. *In this photo, taken in the 1920s, the building on the right is Ann Pareil's restaurant, in 1883 it was the Truman-Verutti House. It is now a commercial store, as is the building next to it. The last space, which was built in 1857, has been Richard Gularte's real estate office for more than thirty years. No. 318, on the corner, was built in 1860 and housed the town's first justice court. More recently it has been a bakery and delicatessen.*

The Crane House, located on the corner of Polk and Second Street, was built in 1835 and may be the oldest remaining house in California to have been built by Americans. Originally, part of it was the Ox Cart Tavern. Encarnacion Ortega Crane lived here from 1857 until her death in 1894. The house has remained in the Crane family and is now owned by William Crane Roddy. The photo on the left was taken in 1938 and the other after recent restoration.

39 Washington Street. *Steve Lavagnino built this Queen Anne cottage at Fourth and Washington streets for his wife in 1906 when she refused to live in the upper floor of Tuccoletta Hall after the 1906 San Francisco earthquake. The house is now used commercially.*

104 The Alameda. *The Old Brewerey building, built in 1871, is now a private residence.*

The Library Association was granted free use of a room for six months in 1897.

There were more problems as the town and the times progressed, and changes became necessary, such as checking the cost of "installing water and patent closets downstairs" (1906) and installing acetylene lights in all downstairs rooms (1907).

This unusual source affords an opportunity to see how one group was affected by and responded to the changing economy of San Juan during its early years.

Additional entries in the twentieth century were of more internal and fraternal interest.

San Juan Centennial

There was a real home town celebration September 6 and 7, 1969, and home town it should be because it was a centennial observance of the incorporation of the town of San Juan in 1869.

Headquarters of the 1969 Centennial Historical Committee was in the city hall, with Ray Gervais as chairman.

A two-day celebration was planned, and the *Mission News* joined the celebration with an oversize issue devoted to a brief history of the town, the history of active service organizations, and a guide to the two-day event.

Mayor Leonard Caetano launched the celebration at two o'clock on Saturday, September 6. Caetano received early experience at speaking at festivals when, thirty-six years earlier, at the age of ten, he was called upon to speak before one of the pageants. It is certain he spoke many more times at opening ceremonies during his record sixteen years as mayor.

The old Town Hall and Fire House shown from the Second Street side in a photo taken in 1948.

The town's current City Hall was built in 1957. The building was donated to the city by Mr. and Mrs. Arthur S. Nyland to memorialize their son, Robert Nyland, who was killed in World War II. A portion of the building was used for several years as the post office. The city's fire equipment is housed in the rear.

The Boy Scouts and Girl Scouts also participated in opening ceremonies at the two-hour program. Pete Sutti was master of ceremonies.

As at other festivals, Sunday's program began with a parade. Unlike the usual parade, however, this one was history-centered. Many entries featured people dressed in historic costumes, in buggies or wagons, on horseback, or walking.

Among other events throughout the day there was a chicken barbecue by the volunteer fire department, an open house at the city hall, doughnuts and coffee for twenty-five cents at the I.O.O.F., and tamales and salads served by the Guadalupe Society in the mission arcade.

A major display was a collection of pictures by the San Juan Bautista Historical Society. The society sold books it had printed two years earlier with over twenty-five pictures from its large collection.

A smaller book was published as a centennial souvenir by the centennial committee, with pictures from the society and *Mission News*.

The evening offered a varied program beginning with square dancing from seven to eight o'clock, fireworks from eight to nine, and a dance from nine to one-thirty in the morning.

In the special September 5, 1969 centennial edition of the *Mission News*, editor Edward R. Lamb, familiarly known as Ed, gave an outline of his thirty-five-year tenure with the newspaper:

"Your present editor and publisher came to San Juan Bautista in June, 1931, and with the exception of eight months working as a linotype operator in Palo Alto in 1934, has been here ever since.

"I worked part time for the News under Mr. and Mrs. Roy Slater; part time for Anderson pear orchard, and part time as a shoe salesman and clerk at Penney's in Hollister, before taking over the paper here in 1934.

"The assistant editor, printer's devil and all-around everything in the plant is Marj, a 1940 import from the bright lights of Hollister." (Marj was his wife.)

This does not hint of a farewell, but it was less than three months later when he announced in a short article that people were reading their last issue of the *San Juan Mission News*. He gave no reason for his action.

Ed Lamb had served the community well but personal and business reasons combined to motivate him to close. Other media—radio, television, direct mail, and larger newspapers in nearby communities—were growing competition. And on the personal side, he was offered a job at his trade in Salinas which may have looked like a secure haven.

Lamb must have been gratified that he had outdistanced a serious competitor that came to town just a year earlier. Jon Frost arrived in town and launched publication of another *San Juan Bautista Echo* on August 31, 1968.

Frost arrived with a "giant press," a modern piece of equipment for producing an attractive newspaper with many photographs for both news and advertisements. His operation lasted until May 21, 1969.

With all that, the city of San Juan Bautista—the City of History—moved into its second hundred years.

Joseph Cravea arrived in San Juan in 1906 and opened a shoe repair store at 302 Third. It prospered and he added retail shoes and some clothing through the years. In 1919 one of his sons made local history when he went across the street to make the first deposit in the San Juan Bautista National Bank. The family picture dates to about that year. Son John Cravea (below) continued the business and the store became probably the most photographed business in town, but not because the store has lasted nearly ninety years. It is because the bench in front of the store has been dubbed the "Liars Bench" by local folk. Of course it's not that the regulars at the bench are liars.

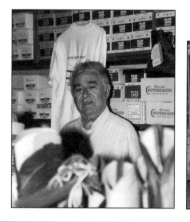

It's just that they like to exchange stories of the past and occasionally some may exaggerate a bit.
The store has no decorated store windows. San Juan residents know what they want, and they know they can come in and find it.

After the *Mission News* was discontinued there were two efforts to replace it. Over a year later, on January 23, 1971, the *Hollister Free-Lance* added a section once a week called "Voice of San Juan Bautista." It continued about six months.

Later the *Pueblo News* was published, with editorial content directed at visitors to the town, but it too lasted only about six months.

Bicentennial Observance

San Juan Bautista participated in the national bicentennial observance of the founding of the United States very much as it did in the two big wars: with wholehearted patriotic support.

Local performance earned the city the coveted honor of being named a Bicentennial City, a title it could use with pride on all official correspondence.

The major event, at least in the number of participants, was a grand costume bicentennial ball. Hundreds of people, all in costume of bygone days, overflowed the dance hall.

Many organizations had special speakers or programs during the year. The largest in terms of the number attending was the annual Festival Rodeo, where a special, impressive, mounted presentation of the colors thrilled the thousands of observers.

The community also participated in the statewide observance by joining in the Bicentennial De Anza Trek. Mounted men and women, in relay teams, carried a leather pouch containing bicentennial documents along the discovery trail to San Francisco Bay created by the Don Juan Bautista de Anza party in 1774.

Armand Holthouse led the San Benito County relay team that brought the pouch from Monterey County on June 25, 1976.

A local gathering welcomed the team on the plaza in observance of the contribution of de Anza and others like him for the progress in the West. The team then took the pouch to Gilroy, Santa Clara County. The national observance touched many people in the Centennial City of San Juan Bautista.

1976 BICENTENNIAL FESTIVITIES

The 1976 San Juan Bautista Rodeo dominated the local national bicentennial observance. A huge crowd of 9,478 turned out. Opening ceremonies featured a replica of the 1776 Liberty Bell with Monsignor Amancio Rodriquez, mission church pastor, making the welcoming address.

The 1976 Fiesta Rodeo parade was led by a Wells Fargo stagecoach with Virginia Fellengham driving. Next to her is Leonard Caetano, mayor and Fiesta Rodeo chairman.

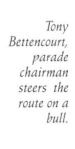

Tony Bettencourt, parade chairman steers the route on a bull.

Armand Holthouse, San Benito County leader of the Bicentennial De Anza Trek leads local horsemen as they arrive from Monterey County.   Photo: courtesy A.G.A. Balz

LIBRARIES & SAN JUAN BAUTISTA

Libraries have been a pride and a concern of the mission, the town and the park service in San Juan.

An inventory of the mission library in 1835 showed that it was the third largest in the twenty-one California missions. There were 183 books valued at $591.00, a sizable investment at that time. There is still a substantial library for the use of the mission staff, and many books are sold in the mission gift shop.

Carl Martin Luck's prosperous gas station was right at the main turn off of old Highway 101.

The Carl Martin Luck Library was given high priority after Miss Francesca Luck bequeathed the land to the city.

All through the early years of the town of San Juan, the trustees allowed money for a library, usually specified for rent.

In the 1880s a Library Auxiliary was founded by the residents of the community. It met weekly in members' homes and collected books to be loaned out.

In the 1890s the Masonic lodge provided a room in its building for a reading room. Initially it was free but later a nominal rent was charged.

With the coming of the twentieth century, the town board of trustees, reflecting the spirit of the times, passed Ordinance 15, providing for the San Juan Public Library. Taxes and a board of library trustees were all provided for. The ordinance was passed November 7, 1905.

The following March all details had been cared for, so the library trustees delivered an "inventory of fixtures, regulations that had been adopted, and a deed" to the town trustees. These were accepted, and Miss Breen (not further identified) was appointed librarian at pay of ten dollars per month. This information was written above a copy of the published ordinance.

Despite the formal organization provided in the ordinance, the auxiliary's old minutes show that they were often called upon for assistance. In 1908 rent was three dollars per month, and for a time borrowers of books were required to pay ten cents per month. The following year, "due to lack of funds," the city asked and the auxiliary paid thirty-five dollars rent and a delinquent light bill.

Through the years the Library Auxiliary continued to support the library with books, money, time, and work. Many individuals also helped, but none of them ever dreamed of the good fortune that was to befall the town in 1974.

One might say the good fortune dated to the previous year because that was when Miss Francesca Luck wrote her will. It was not until after her death, May 26, 1974, that the San Juan City Council learned that Miss Luck had left a square block of land to the city of San Juan.

Miss Luck specified that the land be given to the city with the stipulation that "a public library, public museum and park" be built there "in memory of Carl Martin Luck," her father.

The property is bounded by Third, Monterey, Second and Tahualami streets. Miss Luck owned another parcel at Third and Polk streets, which she said should be sold and the money used for taxes, expenses and development of the city block.

A citizens advisory committee to the Luck Property Project was appointed. On March 8, 1976, it reported to the city council that favorable seismic reports had been completed. The town trustees voted to go ahead, and soon architect Richard K. Rhodes was at work on plans. The Cullumber Construction Company submitted the low bid of $106,638 for the building, which was called phase one of the project.

COMMUNITY SPIRIT

any community projects and service organizations in San Juan Bautista reached a terminal point by the 1970s. Others are ongoing.

The Texas Lodge Masons No. 40, founded in 1853, was the first fraternal organization in San Juan. The second fraternal organization, which remained active until recently, was the International Order of Odd Fellows, usually called I.O.O.F. Organized April 30, 1869, the local lodge was the San Benito Lodge No. 159 of San Juan. It celebrated its centennial with the city, but by the early 1980s it sold its building at Third and Polk streets and the remaining members transferred to the Hollister I.O.O.F. lodge.

The Harmony Club was reported to have been a popular social group in the last decades of the nineteenth century. The San Juan Brass Band was the musical group mentioned as playing at most socials, balls and civic events from 1870 to 1900.

In the revived spirit of the first decade of the new century two new clubs were formed. The first was a San Jose group called the Fremont Memorial Association. Its goal was to organize patriotic events eulogizing the role of General John C. Fremont as leader of military activities in the area that were important to the state and nation.

A special flag raising event on the plaza was organized in 1906. This had special meaning because Fremont was responsible for two flag raisings in San Juan in the Mexican-American War.

It was in March 1846 that Fremont was credited with raising the first flag of the United States over California land. This was on Gabilan Peak (later renamed Fremont Peak) when General Castro was attempting to drive the Fremont company out of the area.

The second flag raising was the focus of the 1906 event. A replica of the 1846 flag was raised on a special pole made by the association and placed on the spot where Fremont's flag was placed on June 17, 1846. Fremont followed General Castro's demoralized troops retreating from Monterey. Fremont raised his flag in front of the building that had been Castro's headquarters. He considered this the end of hostilities in Northern California.

While the association is no longer active, it gave rise to another group that has been most active through the years, the local parlor of the Native Daughters of the Golden West.

Native Daughters of the Golden West

A report of the third observance in San Juan in 1908 read: "Past Grand President Eliza D. Keith took part in the raising of the flag by the Fremont Memorial Association, in the plaza of San Juan Bautista, where the flag was raised sixty-two years previously by Captain Fremont."

Ms. Keith had been state leader in 1902 and 1903 of the Native Daughters of the Golden West.

Two years later, on February 23, 1910, the San Juan Bautista Parlor No. 179 of the Native Daughters of the Golden West was instituted. Three months later it was planning participation in the annual June fiesta. Its goal was to buy a bell for the mission.

The Native Daughters have supported many projects throughout the years, and the Fremont observance has continued as a major project.

While the Fremont Memorial Association disbanded, other groups have continued the tradition. One of the most constant helpers has been the local Veterans of Foreign Wars post.

Sometime prior to 1918 the flag raising event was transferred to Fremont Peak. This has continued and has become an annual pilgrimage, usually on the Sunday nearest to March 4.

This hand-drawn parlor seal was reproduced in the Native Daughters of the Golden West Centennial (1886-1986) Record Book.

In 1918 the *San Juan Mission News* reported the earlier treks were undertaken only by people on horseback, but that year, "many went up in autos, which speaks volumes of praise for the county road supervisors; others in carriages and on horseback."

Participants then and through the years since then have come for the pilgrimage from all over the central coast area. The attendance has varied, but in most years participation has been in the two hundred to three hundred range.

A news story of September 9, 1922, disclosed a project about the cross on the hill that has been overlooked in most articles about the historic cross.

The headline in the *Mission News* read, "Native Daughters Have Replaced Old Landmark." The article reports, "...the cross which for many years has been a landmark located on Flint Hill, but was blown down by heavy wind, has been replaced in a substantial manner, D. C. Grosscup having done the job.

"Since the cross was demolished many suggestions were forthcoming from different sources . . . members of the San Juan Parlor took up the proposition, and before the public was hardly aware of the action, the old landmark had been replaced. . . . When asked about the action [one member said], 'We done it all by our own little selves.'"

Members of the Native Daughters of the Golden West worked in many ways to raise money for their projects. The *Mission News* many times would announce one week that the ladies "are going to hold a cooked food sale Saturday afternoon . . . at the Abbe Store; buy, buy, buy!" The women would prepare

ANNUAL TREK TO FREMONT PEAK

An early group of riders ready for the annual trek to Fremont Peak. Begun sometime prior to 1918, the tradition has enjoyed the support of more than one San Juan Bautista service organization.

The flag is raised on the approximate site of the 1846 flag raising.

dishes that needed little more than warming, and apparently the money-raising effort worked. Parlor No. 179 often was listed as having given twenty-five dollars or more, when the names of contributors to the war bond drive were recorded in the newspaper.

A major project was launched in 1935 when the Native Daughters bought the Pico Adobe at 203 Fourth Street. They restored the building, modernized some facilities, and cleared and landscaped the yard, creating a truly historic and yet comfortable meeting place.

The building is one of the oldest buildings in town. One authority arrived at a construction date of 1836. One man favored the 1840s "because the floor joists are sawed timber." Both may be correct; many adobes were built with earthen floors and had wooden ones added later.

Ralph Pico, builder of the house, was a Basque sheep raiser in Mexico and California before coming to San Juan. He was wealthy for that time, and in his declining years he returned to his beloved Pyrenees.

The Town's Own Service Club

In the booming 1920s service clubs were becoming popular in cities large and small. Established clubs would reach out to nearby towns and help them organize a club. Thus, they grew and became national or international in membership.

Several clubs in nearby towns talked to San Juan professionals, businessmen and civic leaders about organizing a club in San Juan. They talked and talked, but the locals were not impressed. In local conversations they talked about alternatives, resulting in their decision that they could just as well organize a local club. This they did and chose the name of San Juan Bautista Service Club.

Their decision resulted in organized assistance to scores and scores of worthwhile community projects.

One of the first projects of the club was an ongoing campaign to place a new cross on the hill known best as Pagan Hill. The San Juan Parlor of the Native Daughters of the Golden West had raised more than half of their budget for the new cross when the Portland Cement Company closed in 1929 at the outset of the Great Depression.

However, the closing of the plant did not stop the company from supplying the cement for the cross. The service club rallied helpers and money for the final push to complete the construction. Through the years club members have had a major role in the maintenance of the cross.

Another continuing project since the club's organization has been consistent support of the Boy Scouts and Cub Scouts.

The club also supported other youth programs, including the development of the playing field south of Fourth Street now known as Abbe Park. In recent years it has been used for softball.

Lauren Verutti Preschool Park on Second Street is one of the numerous projects of the club throughout its thirty-five-plus years.

Somewhat later the service club acquired land on Second Street for tennis courts. It is now equipped for a preschool children's playground and park and is known as the Lauren Verutti Preschool Park. It is maintained by Joel Verutti, the father of the girl for whom it is named. The club has turned both properties over to the city for recreational uses.

The club provided onetime assistance of both money and supervision for a beautification project on Second Street. Three blocks of rock wall and sidewalk were constructed on the Second Street side of the mission property.

Yet another major project was taken over by the service club in 1993 when it assumed responsibility for maintenance, repairs and supervision of the Community Center. Club members began a series of improvements with a complete exterior paint job.

These are just examples of the major projects of the club. There have been many more which also are important to the community. All the club's projects serve as testimony to the validity of the decision made in 1929 to organize the San Juan Bautista Service Club.

City of History's Historical Society

"The City of History" existed for nearly a hundred years without a formal historical society. One hardly seemed necessary as nearly everyone in town was involved in history and rallied around when there was a costume ball or an Old West parade, or when repairs were needed at a historical site, or for other such projects.

When the Rev. Triono wrote the history of the mission in 1914-1918, he told of receiving many gifts for a museum. The town was very conscious of the moniker "The Little City With A Big History," as it was called in the 1920s. In about 1930, while planning for a special fiesta, Mayor Abbe said he had a collection of memorabilia intended for a museum that he hoped to see established in the Castro-Breen house.

The longer nickname was shortened in later years until "The City of History" was officially adopted.

In 1965, a group of history-minded people decided that an organization was needed, and the San Juan Bautista Historical Society was organized as a California corporation with tax-free, nonprofit status.

The first project undertaken by the society was the purchase of the Old Settler's Cabin from William G. Mackenzie in 1966. The cabin was given to the State Historic Park.

In 1967 the efforts of the society were primarily devoted to supporting a project of renovation of the Plaza Hotel.

A second project that year was the publishing of *Historic San Juan,* Volume I, which presented twenty historically important pictures in large format. Each is identified in a concise historic legend.

The enthusiastic reception of the book prompted the society to publish Volume II two years later. This volume had a different assortment of pictures and was one of the souvenirs for the town's centennial observance. During the year the city appointed the historical society to the Community Advisory Board.

In 1968 about two hundred people joined the society members at a dedication of a plaque memorializing Patrick and Margaret Breen's family. A committee was assigned the task of finding some-

one to write a history of San Juan's volunteer fire department, and another to persuade Wells Fargo to build a replica of the building which housed its stage stop, telegraph office, shipping facility, and money changing and other minor services.

In 1969, the society submitted a plan to the State of California for the gardens of the State Historic Park.

The society's publication committee chose about twenty pictures to add to its 1970 reprint of the memoirs of Isaac Mylar, *Early Days at Mission San Juan Bautista,* originally published in 1929. Valley Publishers of Fresno, owned by the author of this book, published the 1970 reprint. Several printings of the book have been issued since then. Valley Publishers reprinted three other books of the area, including *East of the Gabilans* by Marjorie Pierce in 1976. The society hosted a book-signing reception for the author that drew nearly four hundred people.

In 1970, the society supported the designation of Old Stage Road and Salinas Grade Road as scenic highways. Regarding the routes of local roads, the society urged that no interchange be included at the intersection of Highway 156 and the Alameda.

In the early 1970s the society took a constructive stand on several community projects. It supported the closing of the Plaza to traffic; assisted in the design and setback of the new Bank of America building; urged better treatment and care of the Indian village site at Second and Franklin streets; and pressed for completion of the restoration of the Plaza Hotel.

In this period the society also aided in the restoration of the Glad Tiding (Congregational) Church building, and lent shutters for several old buildings on Third Street.

In 1973 the society purchased the Jim Jack Cabin and donated it to the State Historic Park.

From 1972 to 1974 the Luck Library Project, begun with a bequest by Francesca Luck, received continuing support at all levels. The most substantial support was the funding of one-half the purchase of a microfilm viewer and copier. This equipment was essential for library patrons to read the newly-acquired microfilm copies of the 1912 to 1969 *San Juan Bautista News.* Some early copies are missing but overall 98 percent of the papers were microfilmed. In addition to this valuable holding the library has received other microfilm records of historic importance.

The continuing enthusiasm and devotion of the members San Juan Bautista Historical Society augurs well for the preservation of the historic wealth of San Juan Bautista.

Teatro Campesino of San Juan Baustista

San Juan Bautista's Hispanic heritage was greatly augmented by the arrival in 1971 of El Teatro Campesino.

The theater group had been organized only six years earlier in Delano. There they had a large audience of *campesinos* (farm workers) for whom they wanted to present theater, of them and for them. Within a couple of years they moved to Del Rey near Fresno, and on New Year's Day 1969 they moved to Fresno.

In Fresno they found university students eager to participate in staging plays in art form about Mexican folklore, *campesino* life-style and social attitudes affecting their lives.

During this period El Teatro also had units traveling throughout the Southwest. They proudly raised the banner of Aztlan before an ever-expanding audience of students, professors, union officials, farm workers and their families.

Tours have remained a standard annual project of El Teatro with ever-widening borders which have extended even into Europe for several successful tours.

El Teatro was recognized as a serious art form of theatrical production by 1983. *Corridos*, a new folk musical by Luis Valdez, was introduced in April of that year and received rave reviews in both the *San Francisco Chronicle* and *Examiner*. Across the bay the *Oakland Tribune* said, "The success of *Corridos* in San Francisco established a model for launching plays from San Juan Bautista into the commercial marketplace."

Two years later El Teatro celebrated its twentieth anniversary. The highlight of this observance was a banquet in San Francisco where Mayor Dianne Feinstein awarded the first Feathered Serpent Award to El Teatro on behalf of the city and county. Mayor Tom Bradley of Los Angeles set aside the day as El Teatro Campesino Appreciation Day. By this time the organization was receiving financial support in government grants.

About twenty-five large corporations were recognizing the artistic value of El Teatro with regular grants.

When the headquarters of El Teatro was moved to San Juan Bautista in September 1971, it was first located at La Calavera, a small melodrama theater, later a part of Jardines de San Juan Mexican res-

Luis Valdez is the founder and artistic director of El Teatro Campesino. The playhouse and headquarters of El Teatro Campesino is at 705 Fourth Street. The company is committed to developing new contemporary works and theater artists to maintain its tradition in Spanish language theater. His wife, Lupe Valdez, is an actress, a member of the board of directors, and supervisor of the company's bookkeeping. She has toured with the company in California, the Southwest, Mexico and western Europe, including the World Theater Festival in Nancy, France. Both Valdezes are graduates of the California state universities, he in San Jose and she in Fresno.

taurant. The company had been invited to town by Manuel Santana, owner of the Calavera facilities.

Valdez likes to say that his interest in theater really started when he was in the first grade in Delano. He had the honor of playing a monkey in a skit entitled "Christmas in the Jungle."

Valdez's career soared in 1977 when he wrote "Zoot Suit." It broke attendance records in Los Angeles, played on Broadway in New York City, and was made into a successful movie.

This provided Valdez with opportunities to work on movies in Los Angeles, but he did as much of his work as possible in San Juan. He said, "My roots are in El Teatro and I don't want to leave it. And my family is a big priority. San Juan Bautista is a good place to raise a family." He views much of his work as "a new way of looking at California history."

El Teatro refers to its early years, 1965-1970, as the "Flat Bed Truck Years." Valdez later bought a large packing shed, and 1980 to 1985 were the "Packing Shed Playhouse Years" for the theater group.

All the years have been growth and progress years, and Valdez never fails to share credit with "a key staff" of usually about six specialists, a "core company" of about fifteen, and "associates" of a variable number.

Every December there is always staff enough in town to perform traditional Christmas pageants in the old mission church. Las Posadas is El Teatro's least publicized contribution to the community and, for many, its most appreciated.

JACL in San Juan Bautista

Unlike the Mexicans and Spanish who were the original immigrants to the area, unlike the Europeans who came for the Gold Rush or to escape oppression, unlike the Chinese who were brought as early as the Gold Rush to do heavy work, the Japanese came at a relatively recent date. Except for very few, they were twentieth-century immigrants.

In the early 1880s the Chinese population in California dropped and farmers feared a shortage of dependable workers. They looked to Japan for help, but by 1890 there were only twenty Japanese in Monterey and Santa Cruz counties.

The number of Japanese grew slowly, and by 1910 there was a small Japantown at the south end of Third Street or the Alameda. In the vicinity was a fish market, tofu factory, store, hotel, pool hall, and Chinese gambling hall.

The national immigration laws prohibited the Issei (first generation) from becoming American citizens. In 1913 the California legislature passed a law prohibiting the Issei from buying any land.

Sandy Lyndon, a professor of history at Cabrillo College and the author of *Fools Gold*, a history of the Chinese in the Central Coast area, wrote a brief history of the Japanese in the area for the JACL's (Japanese American Citizens League) program at the time of the group's fiftieth anniversary in 1985. Dr. Lyndon's history is the basis for much of this article. Quotations not otherwise credited are from his history.

Many Issei feared that the Japanese would never be permanent so they trained their children, Niseis (second generation) in art and language, preparing them to live in Japan.

The Issei could lease land and many did. In 1916 their strawberries grown in San Benito County sold at a premium in the San Francisco market. Their children who were born here were American citizens and could buy land, which some did.

During World War I the *Mission News* published a list of donors to war drives; many dollars were contributed by the Japanese.

In 1924 immigration stopped completely under an Immigration Quota Act. Enough women had come by then so the Japanese community was well established and family-based.

The Japanese community built a building on First Street in 1930. It is often called their school house but was designed to be a social center. After the war some families lived there briefly while waiting for the return of their land. Since then it has been used for community functions.

In the twenties, the Japanese Americans began to feel more secure and see themselves as a permanent part of the whole community. They had their own club, known as the Friendship Club, the forerunner of the Japanese American Citizens League in this area. The first use of the name JACL was in San Francisco, and in the spring of 1935 local Nisei conferred with that group. Upon their return they met in the Japanese School of San Juan Bautista and agreed to form a local JACL. The first official meeting was held June 22, 1935.

The late thirties was a most congenial period. The *Mission News* allotted space every week for Japanese news submitted by Kay Kamimoto. The "local JACL gained strength and direction . . . scope widened to include public service projects and political issues." The JACL contributed to hospitals, charities and community activities.

In June 1941, the JACL was for the first time invited to enter a float in the annual San Juan Bautista Pageant parade. The club's entry won first prize of ten dollars in cash, a nice amount in those days.

War ended all this.

Although there was no evidence of conspiracy, federal authorities considered the Issei to be enemy aliens, and locally many were jailed. The Nisei and JACL had to take charge. They decided in this area that as good American citizens they should obey the law. This meant that in about four months local Japanese would be evacuated to a center away from the coast, in this case to a camp at Poston, Arizona. For three years they lived in Poston Area I, Colorado River Relocation Center.

They maintained a normal life in camp as best they could. The local JACL functioned as a leadership unit. It was the only chapter that was active in the camps. While at Poston some Niseis arranged to go to middle western or eastern cities. When the war ended less than half the Japanese returned to this area.

The JACL returned to San Juan and adopted a program that included a "most consistent and pervasive work in the area of education." It sponsored the showing of the movie *Go for Broke*, about the Japanese American 442nd Regimental Combat team on the European front. It also gave books to schools which would give students a better understanding

of history and sponsored speakers to do the same in the community. The JACL returned to the San Juan Pageant parade and in 1953 won a prize with its float.

The Japanese in San Benito County numbered 526 in 1940 but the postwar census was never more than 142, the number reached in 1980. In 1983 a

A Japanese dinner served at the Kemp Ranch in 1916. Nearby diners, clockwise, are Mrs. Steve Lavagnino, Mr. Lavagnino, Frank Avilla, Sr., Mrs. Avilla, and Mrs. Ben Ahern.

JACL member, John Kurasaki, was elected president of the San Juan Bautista Chamber of Commerce. Kurasaki was the owner of the Mission Farm RV Park. When the JACL planned a celebration of its golden anniversary in 1985, he opened his place for the headquarters and convention center. The event was broadened; in addition to the anniversary it would be the first Poston Camp reunion. The latter was so popular that more reunions were held around the state.

For the reunion in San Juan the board of supervisors of San Benito County wrote:

"Your organization has been responsible for many community activities in our county that have made our county a better place in which to live. Your examples of true citizenship are among the highest on record.

"Again we thank you for what your organization has done and we know your success will continue."

The Volunteer Fire Department
From a history of the volunteer fire department by Martin Penn, compiled by Edward R. Laverone

On the eastern edge of San Juan, in 1866, a fire broke out and quickly burned to the ground a two-story frame house situated on the Alameda and owned by Madame Pauline Orrey de Massule.

At about four o'clock in the morning of November 1, 1867, a fire broke out at the rear of a merchandise store at the corner of Third and Mariposa streets. It swept westward until it reached a brick building (still standing) at the corner of Third and Polk streets. In its path the fire destroyed the New Idria Store belonging to Daniel Harris ($35,000 damage), Ramoni's grocery store, the International Hotel and livery stable ($12,000 damage), the Fonda Mexicana Restaurant of Dona Guadalupe Cantua de Vasquez ($2,000 damage), Murphy's Bakery and other buildings belonging to Felipe Gardela (valued at $10,000).

These fires apparently inspired action that produced an organization that has served the town for more than one hundred and twenty-five years, the San Juan Eagles Hook and Ladder Company.

On the evening of October 23, 1868, a grand ball and banquet was held in the newly built Plaza Hall. The banquet was given by the Eagle Hook & Ladder Company. Musicians were brought to town for this event, and the banquet bill ran to $240.

The San Juan Eagle Hook and ladder Company's first fire truck was built by W. G. Hubbard in his wagon manufacturing shop, in 1869, at the corner of Second and San Jose streets.

Unfortunately, no records revealed the details of how the Eagle Hook and Ladder Company was organized. Old-timers of San Juan believe that J. G. Beuttler was the man most active in getting it properly organized and equipped. In the 1884 photograph of the fire company, he has a place of honor at the center of the group and wears a fire chief's hat. When he died in July of 1886, he was spoken of as an "honored member of the Eagle Hook and Ladder Company," and the whole fire department turned out in uniform for his funeral.

The San Juan Eagle Hook and Ladder truck, built in 1869 and now on display in the San Juan Bautista Historic Park, is one of the oldest vehicles of its type in the state of California.

Human power rather than horse power was used to propel the truck. Two strips of heavy cloth webbing about twenty feet long formed the central part of a harness that stretched forward from the axle of the truck. At five-foot intervals a four-foot hardwood slat was placed with a catch into which a shoulder strap could be fastened. A crew of sixteen men, ten of whom attached themselves to the front of the vehicle, were required. The crew was led by "wheelers" and "headers."

Four of the men in the ladder crew ran alongside (two on each side) and pushed against brackets placed along the bed of the truck. Behind the truck were two more of the ladder crew who pushed the truck. The truck carried several ladders that were built stoutly enough to hold four or five men of the bucket brigade as they passed water up to the burning roof.

The parts of the truck beneath the bed were once painted a bright red. The bed itself was an azure blue with a white stripe at the top. At one time a gong was attached to the rear axle to ring loudly as the truck moved along the street.

In 1909 the people of San Juan decided to install a public waterworks. Before this, wells, occasionally with windmills above them, were the only sources of water in town.

With the water works came the placement of the hydrants throughout town in the summer of 1909. It was then feasible to purchase a hose cart, which was bought in June from a New York firm for $77.00, with 500 feet of "Dragon Brand" hose at eighty cents per foot and two brass nozzles at $7.00 each.

In January of 1885 the board of trustees decided to move the fire house closer to the center of town. A small lot on Second midway between Polk and Mariposa became its new home.

In 1893 a council room for the city board of trustees was added to the back of the fire house.

In February of 1946, a public auction was held, and the old fire house was sold to the highest bidder for $375.00. It was torn down two years later to make way for a new fire department building. The bell turret stood for a few years longer until the new fire house was built on the site in the spring of 1957.

As fire companies around the Monterey Bay area became more efficient and better equipped they developed a fierce pride in their individual abilities. This led to friendly competition at regional tournaments.

The San Juan Eagle Hook and Ladder Company with trophies won at Watsonville in 1884 and at Santa Cruz in 1882. The date of the picture is not otherwise established.

The first organized tournament in this area was held at Watsonville in 1880. Six hose cart teams and one hook and ladder team demonstrated their skill in using their equipment and were timed according to a set of predetermined fire tournament rules.

The front axle of the hook and ladder truck was placed over the starting line. At the sound of the starter's pistol ten men in special harness would pull the truck 900 feet to the finish. Three ladder men pushed on either side. A ladder climber rode on top of the truck and about one hundred feet from the finish he would jump off and two of the ladder men, called anchor men, would pull the ladder off the truck, making spikes at the bottom of the ladder sink into the ground at the finish line or just beyond it. When the spikes hit the ground the ladder climber scrambled to the top while the other four ladder men braced the ladder up to a vertical position.

In November of 1881, the San Juan Eagles participated in their first tournament in Hollister. They were beaten by the only other competing hook and ladder company, the "Pioneers" of Hollister, by one-fourth of a second. They had "made splendid time from the start to the finish of the run. However, they made a "balk" with their ladders and received the time of 57¼ seconds! Later, after the winners were announced, "the foremen of the winning teams were hoisted on the shoulders of the mob and carried through the streets. The men congregated in the various saloons, on the sidewalks and street corners and in the most demonstrative manner expressed their satisfaction at the result." (*San Benito Advance*, November 12, 1881)

N.C. Briggs, Esquire, awarding the prizes at the Hollister event of 1881 said, "Nearly all nations and people have favored contests calculated to develop the skill and physical strength of their people. Your contest of skill is that of an advanced and enlightened age. While you seek to develop manhood and become proficient in the performance of your undertaking, it is in the spirit of the honorable duty, and the cause of humanity—the preservation of property and the saving of lives of your fellow citizens—a calling which deserves the highest commendation, the greatest assistance and encouragement from the communities in which you live."

The San Juan Eagles never lost another hook and ladder event to Hollister.

The next tournament was held in Santa Cruz in June of 1882. The San Juan Eagle Hook and Ladder Company entered in this event and won first prize in the hook and ladder competition. The other three hook and ladder companies were the Hollister Pioneers, the Santa Clara Company and the Santa Cruz Company. San Juan won in the "hitherto unequaled time of 51 seconds." The Eagles were awarded a prize consisting of a silver fire trumpet and seventy-five dollars in coin. It was significant to all that San Juan had beaten the fastest time of the late Iowa Tournament by three seconds.

According to the *Advance* "It was nearly five o'clock before the Eagles of San Juan went to the score. This team was the favorite from the start, especially with the ladies, and when they came down the course like the wind, cheer after cheer was heard. It was a pretty run. There was no faltering, no lagging. Every man seemed to understand his business and the full measure of responsibility that devolved upon him. It was a lively pull and a pull all together. The ladder was hoisted without a bobble and the ladder man went up it like a squirrel. The watches of two unofficial timers recorded 52½, another 52¼ and another 52 but the time was given in by the judges as 55½."

The third firemen's tournament was held at Watsonville on May 16, 1884. In spite of a track reported to be "in miserable condition," the San Juan

Eagles won first prize in a run timed at 50¼ seconds. For this, San Juan received "an elegant silver pitcher and goblet" and $275 in coin. The victorious

Old time members of the Eagle Hook and Ladder Company standing in front of the hook and ladder unit in which the team won a world record of 48 minutes in July 1906. They were also leaders in local affairs. The picture is from the 1930s. From the left, William Prescott, Ed Pearce, Luis Raggio, Ernest CC Zanetta and George Abbe.

team took a train to the west end of the San Juan Valley and then rode in a Concord coach to San Juan, an *Advance* article stated.

A brief description of the grand ball at the Plaza Hall which celebrated their homecoming was also given by the *Advance*: "The hall was beautifully decorated for the occasion and after dancing a bountiful supper prepared by the ladies was spread. Many handsome floral pieces were noticeable, prominent among which was a miniature hook and ladder truck presented by Mrs. Windsor to Arthur Graeme, the handsome foreman of the Eagle Hook and Ladder Company."

The 1886 State Firemen's Tournament at Salinas was the last of a series in this locality, but it was perhaps the most spirited tournament of them all.

Having lost the last tournament by one-fifth of a second, the team was determined not to lose again.

The *Salinas Valley Index* reported the event as follows:

"At the flash of the pistol away they flew and in 48¾ seconds afterward Quentin Miranda had his hand on the top rung of the ladder at the outcome, beating the Santa Cruzans by 3/5 of a second. The scene that ensued beggars description. Men shouted and cheered til they were hoarse. Ladies waved their handkerchiefs and parasols and showered bouquets of flowers upon the victors."

The final hook and ladder contest for many years to come in which San Juan participated was held in Salinas on September 9, 1906. The old fire truck had been greatly altered, but spirits were high as ever. Dave Wright, the ladder climber, reached the top of the ladder as the judges' clocks were nearly at the 48-second mark. The final decision, however, gave the flat time of 48 seconds. The Watsonville team came in closely behind with a time of 49¾ seconds.

In 1933 a hose team called the "Dons" organized to represent San Juan at Watsonville's Fourth of July celebration. A nineteen-second delay due "to not being used to the methods," the *Mission News* reported, "was just the time by which they missed first place." They did bring home a fifty-dollar prize, however.

The "Dons" continued in competition for two more years. San Juan's hose cart and hook and ladder truck were loaned to the San Juan Bautista State Park, where they are now on display for all to enjoy.

In the spring of 1918 the board of trustees asked Ernest CC Zanetta and Joseph De Lucchi to reorganize the fire department. This they did, and by 1921 the fire department's first motorized fire truck was in use.

Since 1868, the firemen have had at least one grand ball a year. The purpose of this event was not only to have a good time but also to raise money to buy new equipment. The ball was originally held at the Plaza Hall, where the dance floor was considered one of the best in the state. The ball is now held at the Veterans of Foreign Wars hall on a Saturday close to Saint Valentine's Day.

One brief newspaper article appearing in the *San Benito Advance* in March of 1893 gives a fair idea of the commotion that a fire caused: "John Chalmers' incubator, near the cemetery, caught fire at 8:00 p.m. Wednesday evening. The red glow overhanging the town emptied houses of their occupants. The merry-go-round was deserted. The dancing school hurried to the scene. A prayer meeting being held at the Congregational Church did not even

wait to say the usual amen. The Hook & Ladder Brigade responded promptly, but owing to the distance, their services were not needed. One hundred and fifty chickens were cremated."

The volunteer firemen have had a reasonable number of fires in the twentieth century, but the loss level has been low.

WHERE DID THE LADDERS GO?

During the latter part of the 1880s the fire company began to have difficulties with the fire equipment. It seems that the ladders and other equipment were being borrowed at the will of the town's citizens, who were not careful about returning these items to the fire house. As a result, every once in a while the board of trustees would appoint themselves as a committee to find and return the ladders to the fire house. The trouble continued well into the 1890s, and in June 1897 the trustees passed an ordinance that illegal use of fire equipment would be fined five dollars or five days in jail. This seemed to remedy the situation.

The fire that had the greatest potential for a major disaster was reported at 5:30 p.m. on July 8, 1935. This fire began when five tenants of the Flor de Italia Hotel were heating up their dinner of enchiladas and tamales. The small cook stove they were using wasn't putting out much heat, so one of the men, being hungry and impatient, decided to add gasoline to the fuel for the stove. This did not work too well, as an explosion and fire resulted. The men were lucky to escape with only minor burns. Upon learning that Fire Chief Carlos "Cart" Ramires was out of town, Mayor George Abbe along with Ernest CC Zanetta took charge of the fire fighting.

The weather conditions that evening were very windy, and as the fire raged out of control, sparks began to fly and threaten other buildings. The Gilroy Fire Department, the Watsonville Fire Department, and the San Benito County rural fire truck also responded. The Hollister Fire Department headed to help, but returned en route when they were notified that the fire was being brought under control. These fire departments, along with every adult male in San Juan Bautista, fought the blaze for almost two hours before it was brought under control and eventually extinguished.

The high winds and flying sparks that prompted this immense turnout threatened the Plaza Hotel, Breen Adobe, and the building later known as the Morra Hotel and liquor store. The Zanetta Garage and the Breen barn were damaged by flying embers igniting their roofs. These fires were extinguished by men atop the buildings using water packs to douse the flames.

This fire had the potential to be the most destructive fire in the history of San Juan Bautista, but the quick response by the volunteer firemen and all the citizens of the community saved the downtown area. Fire warden H. E. Wyman was quoted as saying after the fire, "I have never seen such a fine bunch of volunteer firemen."

THE STATE PARKS

San Juan Bautista State Historic Park
Fremont Peak State Park
A vision fifteen years to reality, 1919-1935

hen entering the Plaza of San Juan, "at one stroke you are transported into another time and another world. Here in the range of a single glance is epitomized the course of a century and a half of California history."

This was not in the exuberant days of 1907. It was 1919 when an architect, Irving F. Morrow, wrote an article that appeared in the nationally circulated magazine *Architect and Engineer*. His was not the only voice at that time to recognize the unique combination of beauty, history and enduring potential in the San Juan Bautista mission and town.

A planning consultant from Sacramento speaking on San Juan Bautista's potential saw it as a site for two nearby resorts. The pastor of the mission church from 1914 to 1918 was so impressed that he wrote a history of over twenty chapters that was published serially in the *Hollister Advance*.

There were scores of articles about San Juan Bautista in magazines, newspapers and Sunday supplements, all without a town-hired press agent.

While the mission church building was the largest of the California missions, architect Morrow found more to praise, writing, "The church was distinguished by a higher degree of architecture differentiations than any other . . . Its planning is good, its dimensions generous, its proportion noble, and it has been handled with dignity and restraint; and in these it passes the essential requirements of good architecture."

Although the author found the mission most interesting, it was not the only legacy of a historic past. Many buildings were clustered around the Plaza, and the numerous old, well maintained homes in the town added to the atmosphere of olden times.

A local news item later demonstrated how information was getting around to the state. A Southern California society woman had heard about the mis-

sion and town and within weeks had written a play based on the San Juan mission. The play, "The Deserter," was staged in Pasadena, where Father McCaffrey saw it and considered it might be used for a pageant at the annual fiesta.

On the local scene the campaigns gained momentum in the late 1920s to win two state parks and one national park for San Benito County.

The campaigns were not competitive between one and the other. It might be said that everyone was in favor of all three, but quite naturally San Juan people were most concerned about their two state parks. The Pinnacles National Monument, which was dedicated in 1908 by President Theodore Roosevelt, had local support for expansion but no major change was made.

In the heyday of the roaring twenties, the State Park Commission set a goal of "making this state the World's Grandest Playground."

In March 1928 the commission invited delegations of twenty-one Northern California counties to present suggestions for the "playgrounds." The meeting was held in the Whitcomb Hotel in San Jose.

Mrs. W. C. Meacham proposed Fremont Peak as a park site which would be both scenic and historically important. Attorney George Moore, president for twenty-four years of the Fremont Memorial Association, outlined the patriotic significance of the site.

They received enough encouragement to contact owners of the land, establish the appropriate acreage, and prepare the information to put before the commission.

Within a few weeks a representative of the park commission, Mr. Stevens D. Balch, came to see both

Please note: The policy of the State Park Commission in the 1930s was to call a state park within a city a state monument. The San Juan Plaza was the only one in the state at the time it was established. To avoid confusion we have used the present title, "park," at all times. The name now is San Juan Bautista State Historic Park.

the Fremont Peak and Pinnacle sites. Mr. W. I. Hawkins of Hollister showed them to him. Hawkins was dedicating his full time to promoting the three parks for San Benito County.

Mayor Frank Abbe took advantage of the opportunity to show Balch the old Castro Adobe, which Abbe considered to have major appeal as a big museum. Hawkins and Abbe agreed to send all available information on the two park sites to Balch for the commission.

Considering the "world playground" goal of the park commission and the special appeal of the

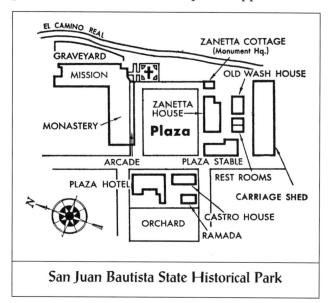

San Juan Bautista State Historical Park

county's sites, local enthusiasts might expect it all to be settled day-after-tomorrow, or at least by next month. It did not work that way.

It was two years before Hawkins arranged a meeting of A. Shepherd of the State Parks Bureau with the land owners on Fremont Peak. The acreage selected was owned by the Portland Cement Company and Dr. Rollin G. Reeves of Salinas.

In the interim, on the national scene the Wall Street stock market had crashed; locally the cement plant had closed; and the state and counties were adjusting budgets to the rapidly changing economy.

But despite all this, the time of the parks was at hand.

The price for the Fremont Peak site of about 100 acres was set at $6,000. On September 19, 1930, the San Benito County Board of Supervisors appropriated $3,000 to match the park commission's share.

Supervisor Fred W. Kemp arranged widening the road to the park to twenty feet. This was not

only for accommodation of tourists but also in anticipation of a record turnout for the annual pilgrimage to the peak the first Sunday in March (1931).

Plans progressed on the state park in town. In May of 1931, the park commission received a detailed report compiled at the request of Laura E. Gregory, the commission's secretary, Newton B. Drury and W. I. Hawkins.

The report was compiled by architects Morrow and Morrow, and Emerson Knight, a landscape architect. It was signed by Irving F. Morrow, who twelve years earlier wrote the lengthy article from which we previously quoted. The *Mission News* called the article a "Fantastic Dream" which Morrow was now working to make come true.

On May 8, the *Mission News* reported that W. I. Hawkins and Father Francis McCaffrey made the announcement that the Plaza site had been accepted after a meeting in Sacramento.

"The announcement was made," the report said, "by W. I. Hawkins, this county's greatest booster, who has been giving much of his time and efforts in a successful attempt to make the natural wonders of this county, especially the Plaza, Fremont Peak and the Pinnacles, state and nationally recognized . . . "

There remained many legal details, one of which was the sale of properties surrounding the Plaza to the state. The San Juan Plaza Preservation League said then that it "had most of the land and buildings under option with the balance expected to be signed up within a short time."

At that time the park commission had appropriated $33,000 for the properties with the same amounts to come from local subscription. The park became a reality in the depth of the Great Depression. It must have been a brilliant ray of hope in 1933.

An announcement was front page news in February 1933, when B. J. Ahern, secretary of the San Juan Plaza Preservation League, announced that park officials had been in town and purchase of properties around the Plaza had been finally negotiated.

The properties, still the core buildings of the park, included the Plaza Hotel, owned by Mrs. Fred Beck; the old Castro home, owned by the Breen family; and the Zanetta home, along with the garage building on the corner, owned by Constable Zanetta and his sister, Miss Victoria Zanetta.

John C. Fremont, who liked to be called The Pathfinder, played important roles in the history of the United States, many in and around San Juan. One such incident is the Battle of Natividad. Natividad was the name of an early land grant high in the Gabilan Mountains south of San Juan. The armed conflict there is considered the only Mexican War battle fought in California.

Colonel Fremont requisitioned 500 horses to be delivered to him in Monterey by two units, one from San Jose, the other from Sacramento. The two companies, totaling about 75 men, met in San Juan November 15, 1846 and proceeded over thee mountains to Monterey. With many recent volunteers, they were as unusual as any group ever mustered in one company. The roll included ten Walla Walla Indians, two Delewares, American ranchers, run-away sailors, Negroes, Englishmen and Germans.

General Castro learned of their intent and ordered a unit of his Californians to intercept and disperse the horses. In the first two confrontations four Americans were killed. Three men were dispatched to Monterey and Colonel Freemont led the reinforcements himself. The Californians laid down their arms and left without further bloodshed.

The picture on the right is Fremont's Peak, previously called Gabilan Peak, as seen from near the Fremont's Peak Park's picnic and recreation area.

The names should be well remembered because in the final settlement they discounted their original price by 40 percent. They received approximately twenty thousand dollars. Most of the deeds were filed in 1933, but the last two were not filed until December 1934.

The San Juan Bautista State Historic Park was officially dedicated September 9, 1935, with appropriate ceremonies by state officials and local people. The Fremont Peak Park also was dedicated in 1935.

The *Mission News* undoubtedly reflected public sentiment when it correctly envisioned, "With San Juan having a state park in the center of town, and the Fremont Peak State Park at its very border, visitors from all over the country are expected to visit here in large numbers in the coming years. It will eventually come to pass that all the buildings around the Plaza will be restored to their original likeness . . ."

The forty-page report of the new state park prepared by Morrow and Knight went into greater detail and more vivid visions; landscape architect Knight contributed suggestions for trees, bushes and flowers. Together they had great plans for the park.

AROUND THE
SAN JUAN BAUTISTA PLAZA

The buildings around the San Juan Bautista Plaza are the buildings that are the very essence of the old town. The State Park has labored for over sixty years to rebuild and retain that aura of life from a time gone by.

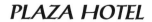

PLAZA HOTEL

The lower floor of the Plaza Hotel was originally an adobe building for Spanish soldiers as early as 1813-1814. In the 1850s Angelo Zanetta acquired the building, reinforced the adobe, and built a frame second floor. Zanetta opened the Plaza Hotel with a grand fiesta. It became known as a congenial hotel with fine food and drink. Changing owners and changing times resulted in gentle aging but its reputation remained untarnished through the years.

The top photo is circa 1919. The two photos of the Plaza's barroom were taken in the 1960s.

CASTRO/BREEN BUILDING

Over one hundred and fifty years old an yet today it looks like it isn't a day over twenty. It was built in 1840-1841 by Colonel Jose Castro to be his house as well as the administrative headquarters of the Mexican government in Northern California when he became governor. The local officials approved of his selection and he was named prefect, but the final approval for a governor had to come from Mexico. Approval never came. Nevertheless, Castro conducted business as a prefect for a time. He later became commanding general of the Mexican forces in Northern California.

After California became a United States territory, he was permanently living here. When the Patrick Breen family came to San Juan after their harrowing experience in the Donner Party, General Castro allowed them to live in his house. They bought it from him in 1848 and used as a hotel during the Gold Rush. One of the descendents signed the deed in 1935 tranfering it to the San Juan Bautista Historic Park.

PLAZA STABLE

The Plaza Stable dates from circa 1870, a time when the horse was king of the roads. That era is recreated by a beautiful assortment of carriages and wagons in the main building. Behind it are workshops for all sorts of repair to keep the horses on the road. Primarily this means stages which were a principal mode of travel and when something was amiss the stage drivers expected an important stop like San Juan to have what was needed to keep them on schedule or at least on the road. Wheelrights, blacksmiths and horseshoers were all there.

PLAZA HALL

This might have become the center of county government if San Juan had become the county seat of San Benito County. That was the goal of Angelo Zanetta who bought this piece of property in 1868. Its adobe origin dated far into the past even then.

Zanetta used bricks to build a two story building designed for county offices on the first floor and a community hall on the second floor.

When the county seat was won by Hollister, Zanetta moved his family into the lower level and the upper one was used for many purposes including dances, grand balls, political rallies, temperence meetings and travelling shows. Many groups used it as a meeting hall, including the volunteer fire department.

Today it beautifully displays the home life of Zanetta's era.

VICKY'S COTTAGE

This building was first built in the downtown area as a Wells Fargo office. Later it was used as a dress shop. In approximately 1885 it was moved to its present location for use as housing for Angelo Zanetta's hotel employees. Angelo's daughter Victoria began living in the building in the 1930s and passed away in the cottage in 1959. It is now used for offices.

SAN JUAN BAUTISTA HISTORIC PARK VOLUNTEER ASSOCIATION

Since before the park was approved, volunteers have played a major role. Volunteers on the State Park Commission met with volunteers from local groups and, with guidance from professionals, brought together a fine, multi-purpose park as fast as financing and staffing permitted.

The names change and the work changes, but through the years there has been a continuing volunteer corps of from seventy-five to a hundred.

Volunteers are able to add to the portrait of the past that the total park successfully replicates. They come not only from the local area but from throughout San Benito County as well as from Monterey County.

As shown here, the camera captures some of their work; other jobs are just as important but not pictorial.

Mother and son visit with a Park volunteer as she uses a spinning wheel to make yarn or thread, possibly for a sock or blouse for the young one. All are dressed as they would have been for such a visit long ago.

(Photo: Floyd Oydegaard, San Juan Bautista S.H.P.)

An outdoors scene, reminiscent of San Juan Canyon when birds and small animals abounded in the area. A hunter with traps at his feet tells how best to use them to add meat or fowl to the dinner table. Of course, there were also destructive varmints that had to be eliminated.

(Photo: Floyd Oydegaard, San Juan Bautista S.H.P.)

A wheelwright shapes a spoke for a wheel of a stagecoach so it can make it over the mountains.

(Photo: Floyd Oydegaard, San Juan Bautista S.H.P.)

A blacksmith pounds out a red hot ring to repair a harness. The coke in the smithy's furnace heats a horseshoe, a ring, or other metal object so hot the smithy can mold it with hammer and tongs.

Volunteers wash, rinse and put the garments through the wringer, just as in days long gone. This is behind the Zanetta House.

A pleasant afternoon is made even more so by a pianist and vocalist. The setting is just as it might have been during the seventy years the Zanetta family lived in the house.

SETTLER'S CABIN

THE FIRST JAIL

The log Settler's Cabin was built in 1843 and is considered typical of homes built for pioneers arriving from the East. It was located on Mission Vineyard Road south of San Juan. In 1966 the cabin was bought by the San Juan Bautista Historical Society and given to the State Historic Park.

The restored cabin was placed at the rear of the former site of the Mission Hotel at Second and Washington streets. A garden setting was added to the cabin, which is in the center of a shaded and convenient rest area.

(Photo from the collection of Mary Poole)

The first jail was built soon after San Juan was incorporated as a town. It was needed, as the closest jail was twenty miles away at first and then seven miles when Hollister became the county seat. This jail lasted more than seventy years and then was replaced by an exact replica that was structurally safe.

RESULTS OF MISSIONARY ACTIVITIES AT MISSION SAN JUAN BAUTISTA IN THE SPIRITUAL ORDER FROM 1797 TO 1832													
YEAR	BAPTISMS		MARRIAGES		DEATHS		NEOPHYTES		EXIST.	CONFESSIONS	COMMUNIONS	VIATICUM	CONFIRMA-TIONS
	Wh.	Ind.	Wh.	Ind.	Wh.	Ind.	M.	F.					
1797	..	87	..	12	..	2	55	30	85	..	..	..	..
1798	1	269	..	58	1	18	176	120	296	..	..	..	..
1799	..	347	..	76	..	51	202	146	347	..	..	..	..
1800	2	641	..	109	..	66	341	240	586	..	..	..	..
1801	..	813	..	148	..	99	428	295	723	..	..	..	..
1802	2	1079	..	206	..	184	507	403	910	..	..	..	..
1803	..	1239	..	258	..	287	522	454	976	..	..	..	..
1804	2	1430	..	329	1	393	550	523	1073	..	..	..	..
1805	..	1647	..	368	..	503	572	540	1112	..	..	..	..
1806	3	1701	1	392	1	703	500	568	1068	..	..	..	..
1807	..	1829	..	418	..	798	..	..	1072	..	..	..	..
1808	3	1856	..	448	2	892	..	470	510	980	150	..	..
1809	..	1886	..	459	..	971	..	..	..	902	12	..	..
1810	6	1915	..	468	2	1055	368	332	700	12	..	..	..
1811	1	1947	..	478	1	1119	354	312	666	37	11	..	..
1812	3	1981	1	494	1	1179	345	293	638	78	12	..	..
1813	1	2028	2	517	4	1231	349	284	633	194	204	..	..
1814	1	2051	1	526	2	1280	330	277	607	189	8		
1815	1	2091	..	537	3	1344	330	250	580	195	23	1	..
1816	7	2147	..	555	2	1400	328	247	575	220	11	5	..
1817	4	2217	2	572	..	1435	346	262	608	399	79	2	..
1818	9	2255	2	591	3	1490	330	252	582	342	48	1	..
1819	6	2407	..	600	2	1561	362	298	660	291	36	2	..
1820	4	2625	1	659	1	1598	442	401	843	280	53	5	..
1821	12	2996	1	747	4	1708	563	535	1098	200	43	9	..
1822	8	3270	3	823	3	1853	621	601	1222	188	51	6	..
1823	10	3396	2	858	1	1942	641	607	1248	206	57	6	..
1824	4	3481	..	881	3	2038	631	590	1221	..	..	..	..
1825	9	3538	..	900	5	2163	618	548	1166	390	30	5	..
1826	7	3626	3	921	4	2257	611	535	1146	296	8	8	..
1827	..	3692	..	935	..	2343	..	..	1108	290	10	2	..
1828	..	378.	.	949	..	2577	..	..	986	200	11	17	..
1829	13	3838	1	962	8	2644	552	417	969	..	..	..	..
1830	..	3896	..	974	..	2697	557	407	964	4	22	..	..
1831	17	3847	3	993	5	2781	531	397	928	210	72	6	..
1832	16	4017	3	1003	..	2854	520	396	916	..	..	..	..

MATERIAL RESULTS AT MISSION SAN JUAN BAUTISTA
LIVE STOCK.—1797 TO 1832.

Year	Cattle	Sheep	Goats	Pigs	Mules	Horses	Total
1797	115	140	...	4	6	21	236
1798	172	499	...	8	5	69	753
1799	253	1108	...	14	5	237	1617
1800	379	2035	...	45	3	329	2791
1801	441	2423	...	50	4	367	3285
1802	618	3800	...	56	6	454	4934
1803	1036	4660	...	22	8	540	6306
1804	1530	5040	...	0	27	1123	7720
1805	...	...	...	...	...	...	...
1806	3100	7200	...	50	35	1600	11985
1807	3700	10000	...	50	30	600	14380
1808	4000	10000	...	48	32	619	14699
1809	5200	7199	...	58	23	457	12937
1810	5600	9630	...	70	37	586	15943
1811	6000	11500	...	81	34	493	18108
1812	6701	11805	...	91	38	593	19228
1813	7500	12000	...	90	34	530	20154
1814	7400	11200	...	66	33	519	19218
1815	8000	13400	...	50	34	588	22072
1816	10000	13000	...	54	33	702	23789
1817	10500	12000	...	33	33	611	23181
1818	10800	12000	...	18	30	537	23485
1819	10000	10100	...	36	22	638	20796
1820	11000	9500	...	30	24	675	21229
1821	11000	11500	...	60	26	794	23380
1822	10200	10000	...	70	30	803	21103
1823	8000	9000	...	50	36	820	17906
1824	8320	9300	...	40	42	808	17510
1825	8224	9367	...	45	44	869	18589
1826	6206	9526	...	46	53	872	16703
1827	6400	10500	...	50	37	682	17669
1828	6000	11871	...	51	18	737	18677
1829	5899	7503	...	40	6	177	13625
1830	...	...	...	...	...	...	...
1831	7070	7017	...	17	6	397	14507
1832	6000	6004	...	20	12	296	12332

MATERIAL RESULTS AT MISSION SAN JUAN BAUTISTA
AGRICULTURE PRODUCTS.—1797 TO 1832.

Year	Wheat Plt.	Wheat Hrv.	Barley Plt.	Barley Hrv.	Corn Plt.	Corn Hrv.	Beans Plt.	Beans Hrv.	Peas Plt.	Peas Hrv.	Total Fanegas Plt.	Total Fanegas Hrv.	Total Bu. Hrv.
1797	...	...	...	...	...	...	...	...	...	...	...	...	...
1798	32	157	4	91	9	5	1	1	1	1	47	285	475
1799	55	241	4	3	1	140	3	20	1	2	64	406	676
1800	64	1010	5	83	4	681	3	21	3	20	79	1815	3025
1801	100	867	6	197	3	150	2	3	1	11	109	1248	2080
1802	52	100	6	100	5	500	3	30	2	3	68	733	1222
1803	118	1200	1	18	3	800	3	30	1	10	126	2058	3430
1804	121	2000	3	41	3	400	3	23	3	25	133	2489	4148
1805	...	...	...	...	...	...	...	...	...	...	...	...	...
1806	150	2420	6	200	3	300	3	30	5	55	161	2805	4675
1807	200	2300	2	300	2	30	1	9	1	5	210	2544	4240
1808	200	2200	6	70	3	100	4	11	4	78	217	2689	4482
1809	200	1309	6	...	6	7	1	1	6	11	219	1398	2330
1810	350	3972	15	254	5	400	3	70	7	270	380	4966	6277
1811	124	857	26	125	12	1000	8	130	9	55	189	2167	3612
1812	118	730	6	72	5	803	5	66	9	84	143	1755	2925
1813	72	1827	6	60	4	300	3	36	8	188	93	2411	4018
1814	29	400	2	30	4	170	2	14	5	126	42	740	1233
1815	40	421	...	...	2	...	2	2	13	155	57	578	883
1816	60	1600	1	14	2	200	2	4	13	24	78	1842	3070
1817	59	1500	...	...	2	337	2	142	3	105	66	2084	3473
1818	77	1872	4	41	2	500	2	144	7	192	96	2749	4582
1819	70	2516	3	116	3	700	5	4	6	93	86	3429	5715
1820	90	2954	7	368	3	884	4	134	2	112	104	4452	7420
1821	58	2957	21	92	3	700	2	103	2	84	68	3936	6560
1822	114	686	...	119	3	70	2	...	2	...	127	875	1463
1823	90	1474	...	704	9	300	3	...	9	...	132	2478	4130
1824	142	3095	5	...	...	...	...	...	...	...	216	3360	5600
1825	106	932	12	420	...	...	2	14	5	76	117	3599	5998
1826	70	439	14	200	3	100	2	10	8	19	157	3705	6175
1827	50	...	29	100	3	80	2	9	10	4	131	1241	2068
1828	...	...	...	...	2	90	4	6	3	7	99	642	1070
1829	...	...	23	255	3	50	...	...	...	...	89	63	105
1830	...	...	...	...	...	...	3	40	...	...	...	...	...
1831	84	840	...	...	4	170	...	...	8	6	122	1315	2192
1832	...	...	...	...	...	...	...	...	...	...	114	1396	2327

BIBLIOGRAPHY

Bancroft, Hubert Howe: *History of California,* Vols. II and III. San Francisco, 1888.

The California Missions: A Pictorial History. Menlo Park, CA: Lane Magazine and Book Co., 1964.

Coy, Owen C. *Pictorial History of California.* Los Angeles, 1925.

—*California County Boundaries, 1923.* Los Angeles, n.p. Revised edition by Valley Publishers, Fresno, CA, 1979.

Elliot and Moore. *History of Monterey and San Benito Counties.* San Francisco, 1882. Reprinted by Valley Publishers, Fresno, CA, 1978.

Englehardt, the Rev. Zephyrin, O.F.M. (Charles Anthony, 1851-1934). *Mission San Juan Bautista: School of Church Music.* Santa Barbara, CA, 1931.

Flint, Dorothy. *Escarpment on the San Andreas: The Probing of a California Heritage.* Hollister, CA: Evening Free Lance, 1978.

Guinn, J. M. *History and Bibliographic Record of Monterey and San Benito Counties.* Los Angeles: Historic Record Co., 1910.

Historic San Juan Bautista, Vol. I and II. San Juan Bautista, CA: San Juan Bautista Historical Society, 1967 and 1968.

Jackson, Helen Hunt. *Glimpses of California and the Missions.* Boston: Little Brown & Co., 1893.

Lydon, Sandy. "The San Benito County Japanese American Citizen League: A Short History." JACL Program for Reunion, 1985.

Milliken, Ralph Le Roy. *California Dons.* Fresno, CA: Valley Publishers, second printing, 1967.

—*San Juan Bautista: The City History.* Los Banos, CA: M and M Printing Service, 1950-1953.

—Numerous notes in Luck Memorial Library, San Juan Bautista, CA.

Mylar, Isaac L. *Early Days at the Mission San Juan Bautista.* Watsonville, CA, 1929. Updated in 1970 and reprinted by Valley Publishers, Fresno, CA and San Juan Bautista Historical Society.

Penn, Martin. *The Eagle Hook and Ladder Company,* and unpublished manuscript prepared for the San Juan Bautista Historical Society.

Pierce, Marjorie. *East of the Gabilans.* Fresno, CA: Valley Publishers, 1977. Subsequent printings by Western Tanager Press, Santa Cruz, CA.

Report on the Historic Resources Inventory of the City of San Juan Bautista. City Cultural Resources Board, 1981.

Souvenir Programs. Mission Centennial Committee (Frank B. Abbe and Nellie Duncan Gleason), June 24, 1897; The Grand Fiesta, 1907; the city's Centennial Committee, 1969.